Interoception: The Eighth Sensory System

Interoception: The Eighth Sensory System

Practical Solutions for Improving Self-Regulation, Self-Awareness and Social Understanding

Kelly Mahler, MS, OTR/L

Foreword by A. D. "Bud" Craig, PhD

©2017 AAPC Publishing
11209 Strang Line Road
Lenexa, Kansas 66215
www.aapcpublishing.net

Publisher's Cataloging-in-Publication

Mahler, Kelly J.

    Interoception: the eighth sensory system : practical solutions for improving self-regulation, self-awareness and social understanding / Kelly Mahler ; foreword by A. D. "Bud" Craig. -- Shawnee Mission, Kansas : AAPC Publishing, [2015]

    pages ; cm.

        ISBN: 978-1-942197-14-0
        LCCN: 2015953302
        Includes bibliographical references.
        Summary: Interoception, a newly identified eighth sense, allows us to "feel our internal organs and skin and gives information regarding the internal state or condition of our body." As such it is also a key component of our emotional experience. This is an area of difficulty for many, including those with autism spectrum disorders. The book reviews the research underlying the effects of poor interoception and outlines strategies for how to ameliorate these effects.--Publisher.

        1. Interoception. 2. Autism spectrum disorders--Treatment. 3. Autism spectrum disorders--Patients--Physiological aspects. 4. Senses and sensation. 5. Sensory integration dysfunction-- Treatment. 6. Sensorimotor integration. 7. Emotions--Physiological aspects. 8. Affective neuroscience. I. Craig, A. D. II. Title. III. Title: Practical solutions for improving self-regulation, self-awareness and social understanding.

QP435 .M34 2015
612.8/233--dc23   1511

Black and white art and Photographs: ©iStockphoto; www.istockphoto.com

This book is designed in Palatino Linotype.
Printed in the United States of America.

Dedication

To the greatest teachers of all, my clients! You inspire me and teach me every single day. And especially to that one client who wisely told me, "People need pushing." You were exactly right! Thanks to all of you for constantly pushing me – pushing me to think differently, pushing me to find a different way, pushing me to see the world differently. This book is for you!

To my husband, daughters, parents and family – your support and encouragement have been unending. I'm so glad that my insula (!) allows me to feel deep love for each one of you.

To my friends – you know who you are. You've given me some of the best ideas contained in this book, challenged concepts that needed challenging and even spent long hours reading parts of this book on beautiful, sunny weekends. I love you.

To Kirsten, the absolute best editor in the world – thank you for everything you have done to turn this dream into a reality.

Table of Contents

Foreword ix

Chapter 1: What Is Interoception? 1
The History of Interoception. 2
Interoception in the Body 5
The Role of the Insula. 6
Behavior and the Urge to Act 9
Self-Regulation 13
Emotional Regulation. 20
Problem Solving 22
Learning About the World. 22
Decision Making and Intuition. 24
Flexibility of Thought. 27
Social Awareness and the Hidden Curriculum 28
Perspective Taking and Empathy 29
Social Touch. 30
Awareness of Self 31
Summary 32

Chapter 2: Interoception & Autism. 33
Interoception, the Brain and Autism 35
Reduced Interoceptive Awareness. 36
Self-Regulation 42
Emotional Awareness. 44
Emotional Regulation. 45
Teaching Self-Regulation 47
Decision Making and Intuition. 48
Flexibility of Thought. 50
Social Awareness and the Hidden Curriculum 50
Perspective Taking and Empathy 51

Social Touch. 52
Awareness of Self 52
Summary 53

Chapter 3: Assessment. 55
The Multidimensional Assessment of
    Interoceptive Awareness 55
The Body Awareness Questionnaire 56
The Toronto Alexithymia Scale. 56
Alternative Methods of Assessment. 56
The Interoceptive Awareness Interview 57
The Assessment of Self-Regulation 58
The Caregiver Questionnaire for
    Interoceptive Awareness 60
Summary 61

Chapter 4: Building Interoceptive Awareness. . .63
Addressing the Underlying Cause. 65
Can IA Be Improved?. 65
Two Types of Intervention for
    Addressing Reduced IA. 65
Adaptations for Reduced IA 70
IA Builders. 71
Summary 89

Chapter 5: A Need for Change. 91

References 93

Appendices
Appendix A: The Interoceptive Awareness Interview . 103
Appendix B: The Assessment of Self-Regulation. 109
Appendix C: The Caregiver Questionnaire for
           Interoceptive Awareness 131
Appendix D: Adaptations for Reduced IA
           – Examples 135
Appendix E: IA Builders – Supplemental Materials . . . 139
Appendix F: Interoception Handout 165

Foreword

We primates are special because at the highest level of our brains there is a complete picture of the ongoing status of our living bodies. This *interoceptive* image of sensory activity represents what is constantly taking place in every organ and every tissue of our body: skin, muscles, stomach, bladder, and even bones and the whites of our eyes. Each of us can feel some of this activity to different degrees; for example, when we feel hungry or when our hands feel cold. Amazingly, our brains use this interoceptive activity to help form all of our feelings – from the feeling of being alive to feelings of love and trust. We believe that these mechanisms evolved because they improve energy efficiency, first in the homeostatic mechanisms that take care of our bodies, and further, in the control of emotional feelings during social behaviors.

In my recent book *How Do You Feel?* (Princeton University Press, 2014), I describe these mechanisms and explain evidence suggesting that the evolution of these processes in humans may have supported the cooperative care of infants and children that some have proposed fostered the emergence of music and language in our predecessors. These are clearly important topics for all of us, yet non-scientists may find it difficult to understand all of the neurobiological findings described in my book, much less in the burgeoning scientific literature that has quickly extended these discoveries.

In this book, Kelly Mahler has distilled what you need to know about these discoveries for everyday life. Here she explains the concept of interoception clearly and accurately, along with new insights into its significance for all of our feelings. She uses these new ideas to provide accessible "brain-based explanations" of common behavioral issues that require interoceptive awareness. These issues affect all of us, and, unfortunately, they often present barriers for individuals with autism spectrum disorder (ASD) that can seem insurmountable. Kelly also shows how these ideas can be applied in direct and sensible ways that can help individuals overcome such barriers by improving interoceptive awareness.

When I first read the draft of the manuscript, I couldn't help but be impressed by her solid grasp of this neuroscientific literature and her intuitive knack for explaining these concepts in language that everyone can understand. I immediately wanted to honor her request that I write the foreword for her book. I am very glad to have this opportunity to encourage readers to absorb her lucid descriptions of these new ideas.

Most important, in this book Kelly gives readers "how-to" guidance for using these ideas to help improve the lives of children and adolescents with ASD by cultivating their interoceptive awareness. Based on her years of experience, she offers practical tools that can be used to guide attention to the messages that our bodies are constantly sending to our brains. We all need to listen to our bodies and understand its messages. She knows how to listen, and she knows how to help others listen better to their bodies. Here she shares her natural understanding of interoception and her recommendations for how we can help others to improve their own interoceptive awareness.

In my humble opinion, this book is an invaluable application of the ideas about how our brains work that I have spent my life uncovering. I truly hope that many readers will find the guidance they need to improve their own lives and the lives of many others by applying what Kelly offers in these pages.

A. D. (Bud) Craig, PhD, is the Atkinson Research Scientist at the Barrow Neurological Institute and is appointed as an adjunct research professor of cellular and molecular medicine at the University of Arizona College of Medicine and an adjunct research professor of psychology at Arizona State University.

CHAPTER 1

What Is Interoception?

We have come a long way from the days when we only acknowledged five basic senses: smell, sight, sound, touch and taste. Now, the vestibular sense – our sense of head movement and balance – and the proprioceptive sense – our sense of our muscles and joints – which were once only discussed within specific fields such as occupational therapy (OT) and neuroscience, are receiving mainstream attention due to their wide-ranging and powerful influence. An increasing prevalence of developmental concerns, such as autism and attention-deficit/hyperactivity disorder (ADHD), are affected by these sensory systems. This has led to greater interest among the general public to understand how our sensory systems influence growth and learning.

Given that well-functioning sensory systems, including the vestibular and proprioceptive systems, or the so-called "hidden senses," are vital to our ability to navigate the world with comfort and ease (Myles, Mahler, & Robbins, 2014), we have spent a great deal of effort to understand each of the seven sensory systems. However, now we realize that these seven systems are not working alone. A fresh surge of research has pushed another hidden or internal sense, an eighth sensory system, into the limelight – **interoception.**

Interoception allows us to "feel" our internal organs and skin and gives information regarding the internal state or condition of our body (Craig, 2002). For example, the interoceptive system helps us feel many important sensations, such as pain, body temperature, itch, sexual arousal, hunger, thirst, heart rate, breathing rates, muscle tension, pleasant touch, sleepiness and when we need to use the bathroom. Interoception helps us sense a variety of general *and* localized feelings, such as feelings of warmth or coldness, tickling or shivering, tension or relaxation, constriction or expansion, sinking or lifting, trembling or steadiness (Craig, 2002; Fuchs & Koch, 2014).

Notably, interoception is a key component of our emotional experience. That is, interoception, or the awareness of our internal body states, is the basis for how we view or feel emotions (Barrett, Quigley, Bliss-Moreau, & Aronson, 2004; Craig, 2002, 2003, 2009; Critchley, Wiens, Rothstein, Öhman, & Dolan, 2004; Pollatos, Gramann, & Schandry, 2007; Pollatos, Kirsch, & Schandry, 2005; Wiens, 2005). For example, before speaking in front of a room full of people, you may feel your heartbeat increase, muscles tense, stomach flutter and a slight overall shakiness. Based on how your body feels at that moment, you might identify that you are nervous. This process happens for many people in a split second and most people do not have to think about it. It happens automatically. This link between clearly sensing body signals and accurately identifying emotions is crucial, for without the body signals it becomes difficult to clearly detect which emotion is currently at hand. Interoception is a vital component to the emotional experience. **Interoception is a vital component to the emotional experience.**

The History of Interoception

The term *interoception* was first coined in the early 1900s by an English Nobel-Prize-winning physician, Sir Charles Sherrington (Sherrington, 1906). Sherrington used the term to refer to the feelings we get from our internal organs. Despite Sherrington's published works, interoception remained relatively unpopular and unstudied for almost 90 years, until a neuroscientist named A.D. "Bud" Craig published a series of papers highlighting his groundbreaking discoveries about the pathways that lead from a wide variety of tissues in the body to specific areas in the spinal cord and eventually land in a specialized area of the brain. Craig suggested that interoception is more than just feelings from our internal organs. **Rather, it is the sense of the entire condition of the inner body, including temperature, pain and itch** (Craig, 2002). Now professionals in many different fields, including neuroscience, internal medicine, psychology and artificial intelligence, have accepted and are studying interoception.

Meet the Eighth Sensory Gang Member!

Hi! I'm Mr. Interoception. I am responsible for helping you feel the inside of your body, including your organs and skin. Check out some of the important information I might tell you, including:

- hunger or fullness
- thirst
- pain
- body temperature
- heart rate
- breathing rate
- social touch
- muscle tension

- itch
- sexual arousal
- nausea
- sleepiness
- tickle
- physical exertion
- social touch
- need for the bathroom

Pay attention to me ... I also give you clues about your emotions. Fast heartbeat, tingly stomach and shaky muscles could mean you are feeling anxious. Slow, rhythmic breathing and loose muscles often signal that you are relaxed or content.

I work closely with my seven friends to help you navigate all aspects of life. Together we make up the Sensory Gang. We are a busy and hard-working bunch!

The Sensory Gang

Ms. Tactile

People say I am so touchy-feely! I can't help it! From head to toe and all over, my skin keeps me "in touch" with the world. Even inside my mouth I feel things – light touch, deep pressure, hard or soft, sharp or dull, vibration, temperature and ohhhhh ... the pain!

Mr. Vestibular

I keep everything "right with the world!" Because of me, you can deal with gravity when you are moving, no matter the direction or speed. Even when standing or sitting still, I am very important because of my sense of balance. Posture and muscle tone depend on the signals I interpret from the inner ear.

Ms. Proprioception

I do more than just push and pull, flex and stretch, pry and press! Information coming from my joints, muscles and tendons helps me adjust my body position for smooth movements with just the "right amount" of pressure. People say I am important for good "motor planning" when this information is accurate.

Ms. Visual

I've got my eyes on you! I am on the lookout to deliver valuable details about what I see. Color, contrast, line, shape, form and movement have a part in how you perceive the world. My messages (with the collaboration of my friends) help determine what to pay attention to and what to ignore as well as help direct your actions and movements.

Ms. Auditory

Do you hear what I hear? I don't mean to whine, but I can get your attention, too. Listen to me, please, I'm all ears. It's not just about volume – consider also tone, pitch, rhythm and sequence of sounds. Processing me can be difficult, but it is necessary if I am to be understood. If I don't have the others help out, I'm just noise ... sigh.

Mr. Gustatory

Ah, to savor the "sweet taste of success," or was it bitter or salty? Maybe sour or spicy? Taste buds and saliva are the grounds for my great sensory contributions. I often get no respect but one thing's for sure, I know "what I like!" By the way, I am intricately linked with Ms. Olfactory.

Ms. Olfactory

Although some consider me not as refined as my other sensory friends, I go way back in time – kind of a survival thing. Strong memories are associated with certain smells. I subjectively consider the odor, especially when Mr. Gustatory is around. Remember, the "nose knows" and … "Don't forget to stop and smell the roses."

Mr. Interoception

Did you feel that? I am responsible for helping you notice the inside of your body. I let you know important things like when you are hungry, full, or thirsty, or when you need to use the bathroom. Pay attention to me … I'll also send you clues about your emotions. Fast heartbeat and upset stomach could mean that you are feeling anxious. Calm breathing often signals that you are relaxed and content.

From Myles, B. S., Mahler, K., & Robbins, L. A. (2014). *Sensory issues and high-functioning autism spectrum and related disorders: Practical solutions for making sense of the world.* Shawnee Mission, KS: AAPC Publishing. Used with permission.

Interoception in the Body

As with all of the other sensory systems, interoception has receptors or specialized cells in specific areas in the body (Table 1.1 provides detailed information regarding the receptor location of each of the eight sensory systems). The receptors take in sensory information from inside *and* outside our body and send these messages to pathways leading to the brain. For interoception, the receptors are located deep within various body tissues, including our muscles, skin and internal organs (Craig, 2003).

The Role of the Insula

The area of the brain that receives most of the information regarding interoception is called the insular cortex, or the insula for short.

The insula uses the information sent from areas such as heart, bladder and stomach and translates the incoming signals into a message that we

Table 1.1
Location of the Sensory Systems

System	Location
Tactile (touch)	Skin
Vestibular (balance)	Inner ear
Proprioception (body awareness)	Muscles and joints
Visual (sight)	Retina of the eye
Auditory (hearing)	Inner ear
Gustatory (taste)	Chemical receptors in the tongue
Olfactory (smell)	Chemical receptors in the nasal structure
Interoception (inside body)	Tissues inside the body including organs, muscles and skin

Adapted from Myles, B. S., Mahler, K., & Robbins, L. A. (2014). *Sensory issues and high-functioning autism spectrum and related disorders: Practical solutions for making sense of the world.* Shawnee Mission, KS: AAPC Publishing. Used with permission.

can identify on a conscious level. For example, the insula may translate the signals into a **body state** such as hunger, thirst, sexual arousal, pain, coldness, etc., or an **emotion state** such as anger, happiness, excitement or fear. In either case, the insula processes the interoceptive signals and allows us to become aware of what we are feeling. **The insula allows us to answer the question, "How do I feel?"** (Craig, 2002).

Key Point

Interoception allows us to experience many important feelings. For the purpose of simplification, these feelings will be divided into two main categories:

1. **Body States**. These involve the basic functions or physical conditions of the body. Body states include hunger, thirst, needing to go to the bathroom, pain, sexual arousal, itch, tickle, temperature (e.g., hot/cold), nausea, headache, illness, muscle tension.

2. **Emotion States**. These involve our moods or emotional conditions of the body. Emotion states include anger, embarrassment, happiness, anxiety, excitement, sadness, fear.

The insula was mentioned as early as 1796 by the German physician Johann Christian Reil. However, because most experts thought it had no major function, no one paid much attention to this area of the brain. Due to the hidden location of the insula deep within the lateral side of the brain (Naidich et al., 2004), it was difficult to study and continued to be misunderstood. With the advent of advanced brain imaging technology, however, we are now able to look deeper into the brain, and with this new ability to study the deep structures of the brain, the insula is emerging as a crucial part of human behavior (Craig, 2009; Kurth, Zilles, Fox, Laird, & Eickhoff, 2010; Uddin, 2015).

A properly working insula leads to better awareness of interoceptive signals. In other words, if a person has a properly working insula, he will likely be more aware of the feelings within his body. Critchley et al. (2004) asked participants in their study to "feel" their heart rate – to identify how many beats they detected without the use of any equipment (a common measure of interoception awareness in research). The researchers found that the participants who were more accurate on the heart rate test also had better activity in the insula. Simply put, the better the insula activity, the better the interoception.

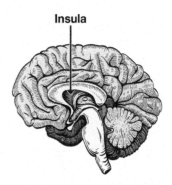

Insula

In addition to activity in the insula, the volume of gray matter in the insula also correlates with good interoceptive aware-ness (IA; Critchley et al., 2004). In simple terms, individuals who are more accurate at feeling interoceptive sensations tend to have thicker insula. Thus, activity *and* structure of the insula are directly related to the ability to clearly perceive interoception signals.

Each person has a left insula and a right insula located deep within the side portion of the brain.

Although we have more to learn, brain researchers now know that the insula plays a vital role in many key tasks (see Table 1.2), the most prominent of which is feeling or detecting the internal state of our body. In other words, the **insula is the interoception center of the brain.**

Researchers are working to gain a clearer picture of the insula and its possible subdivisions as well as its connections with other areas in the brain. For example, evidence suggests that a portion of the insula, the anterior insular cortex (AIC), is part of a brain network called the sali-ence network. In conjunction with a nearby part of the brain, the ante-rior cingulate cortex (ACC), the AIC works to select the most relevant or important sensory information from the massive amount of choices available.

The brain is constantly bombarded by large amounts of incoming sensory information, and the salience network directs our attention to the most relevant or "salient" information. The salience network, when functioning properly, monitors both internal and external sensory infor-mation and allows us to use the most important information to guide our behavior (Menon & Uddin, 2010; Uddin, 2015).

Table 1.2
Factors That Activate the Interoceptive Center
of the Brain (aka the Insula)

Temperature	Cognitive flexibility
Sexual arousal	Emotion regulation
Orgasm	Problem solving
Emotional awareness	Attention to task
Pain	Motivation
Hunger	Intuition
Maternal and romantic love	Decision making
Fight or flight responses	Sensing risk
Full bladder	Understanding norm violations
Thirst	Reading gestures
Disgust over taste and smell	Laughing
Pleasant or sensual touch	Crying
Perspective taking	Coordination of speech muscles
Empathy	Swallowing
Control of urges (e.g., smoking, drug use)	Motor coordination and balance
Control of tics	Sense of self and body
	Listening to music
	Sense of time

Note. This is not an exhaustive list. For full and detailed review see Craig (2014).

Behavior and the Urge to Act

After the brain makes sense of the incoming interoceptive information, it creates a response. **Underlying most of these responses is a goal to reach homeostasis – the body's drive to achieve an optimal internal balance using the least amount of energy possible** (Craig, 2014). The brain is constantly monitoring the incoming interoceptive signals, and when they alert the brain that something is off – the internal balance is off – the brain immediately reacts by sending messages or directions to regain a stable body state or emotion state.

Our bodies are designed to strive for homeostasis on an automatic, *unconscious* level as well as in a *conscious*, purposeful manner. For example, when faced with a situation that evokes fear, the interoceptive sensations set off a series of unconscious, automatic reactions, such as increased blood flow to the muscles, in preparation to attack or run. At other times, interoceptive sensations signal for us to take conscious, purposeful action. For example, if we are thirsty, we are motivated to seek water. If we are cold, we are motivated to seek shelter or warmth. If we are frustrated, we are motivated to ask for help. In other words, these sensations provoke a motivation to behave in a certain way; they provide an urge for action (Jackson, Parkinson, Kim, Schüermann, & Eickhoff, 2011).

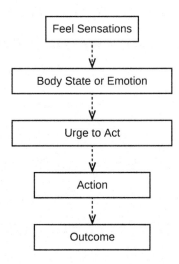

The Urge to Act When Thirsty

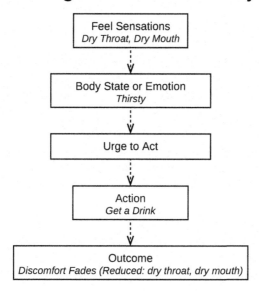

The Urge to Act When Frustrated

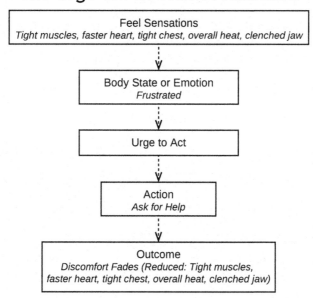

At times, even the anticipation of sensations a future situation may provoke is enough to drive our behavior or urge us to act. For example, when you get ready to go outside on a cold day, unconsciously your body prepares by pumping more blood to certain areas and adjusting your metabolism. In addition, on a conscious level, you might have an urge to put on a warm coat, hat, gloves and scarf. You might even be motivated to start your car in advance so you don't have to endure the cold as long. The anticipation of the uncomfortable interoceptive signals provides a strong urge for action. This urge for action is an attempt to achieve an internal balance or homeostasis.

Similarly, from an emotional standpoint, in anticipation of being nervous during an upcoming job interview, unconsciously your liver releases extra glucose for a boost in energy. On a conscious level, you might stretch and perform deep breathing exercises to get focused and "in the zone." Again, it is all in an effort to reach homeostasis. **The sensations, even anticipation of the sensations, drive the behavior, and provide an urge for action.**

The Urge to Act in Anticipation of Coldness

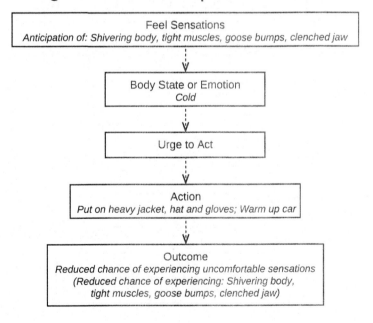

Feel Sensations
Anticipation of: Shivering body, tight muscles, goose bumps, clenched jaw

Body State or Emotion
Cold

Urge to Act

Action
Put on heavy jacket, hat and gloves; Warm up car

Outcome
*Reduced chance of experiencing uncomfortable sensations
(Reduced chance of experiencing: Shivering body,
tight muscles, goose bumps, clenched jaw)*

The Urge to Act in Anticipation of Nervousness

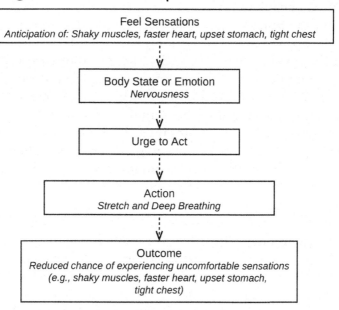

Self-Regulation

When trying to achieve an internal balance, or homeostasis, the behaviors or actions we are urged to use are all a form of self-regulation. Very simply, **self-regulation is our ability to control the way we feel and act.** Successful self-regulation helps us in many ways. For example, it can help us:

- Maintain attention to a task
- Respond to sensations comfortably
- Persist in the face of challenge
- Maintain a feeling of contentment

- Control emotions
- Match energy level to the situation
- Promote healthy behaviors (e.g., eating when hungry, stopping when full; emptying bladder)

The ability to self-regulate is closely tied to our interoception system. That is, interoceptive signals alert us that our internal balance is off and motivate us to take action – to do something that will restore the internal balance. **Thus, the interoceptive system drives our self-regulation behaviors**.

From the time we are born, we begin to develop self-regulation skills (Kopp, 1982). Interoception provides vital information about what is happening inside the body. The sensations are a strong influence on the infant's behavior in the world. From birth, the infant's need for sleep, food, water and warmth is monitored via interoception receptors. In an effort to achieve internal balance, the information drives much of the infant's behavior. In turn, the infant's behavior provides cues to the caregiver on how to help the infant regulate. For example, when the infant is hungry, she cries, and the caregiver feeds her. When the infant is cold, the infant cries, and the caregiver cuddles or swaddles her. The interaction with the care giver helps to reduce the cause of the bodily sensations. At this point, it is co-regulation, as the infant is relying on another person to help identify and adjust her internal system. In the process, the infant is learning valuable information on how to regulate when faced with an imbalanced internal system. Eventually, this repeated practice enables the baby to transition to self-regulation when old enough to begin fulfilling her own needs.

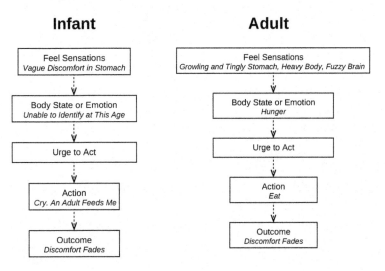

IA is crucial in our development of self-regulation skills. As we grow, we refine this process. Internal sensations become more detailed. We begin to link these sensations with precise body states or emotions. Through trial and error, we learn what action or behavior reduces the discomfort caused by each distinct internal sensation(s).

It is this ability to sense our interoceptive signals that lies at the foundation of self-regulation. Without this information regarding our internal state, without the clear messages that alert us to an imbalance, it is impossible to develop good self-regulation skills. This vital ability to sense our interoceptive signals is referred to as **interoceptive awareness**.

Key Point

Interoceptive awareness refers to the ability to feel the inside of our body with a high degree of clarity and purpose. Good IA involves clearly sensing the signals coming from our internal organs, skin and tissues *and* understanding what these signals mean.

There are multiple subtypes of self-regulation, and all of them are impacted by IA. From being able to control emotions (emotion regulation) to being able to control body states such as hunger or thirst (body state regulation), IA is the vital indicator that the balance is off and it is time to act. Table 1.3 summarizes a few of the subtypes of self-regulation and describes the important contribution of IA to each.

Table 1.3

Role of Interoceptive Awareness (IA) in Subtypes of Self-Regulation

Subtype	Definition	Role of IA
Body State Regulation	The ability to regulate basic body functions or conditions such as hunger, thirst, need for bathroom, temperature. It also includes sensing illness and pain, and managing these states effectively.	Feel hunger sensations, seek food; feel full bladder sensations, seek bathroom; feel pain from a specific area in body, seek help for injury.
Sensory Regulation	The ability to use sensory input to control the way we feel.	Feel discomfort from crowd, seek solitary break; feel distracted by background noise, seek quiet or remove noise; feel comfort from firm hugs, seek when upset.

Table 1.3 (*continued*)
Role of Interoceptive Awareness (IA) in Subtypes
of Self-Regulation

Subtype	Definition	Role of IA
Attention Regulation	The ability to maintain focus and attention to a given task.	Feel distracted by background music, turn off; feel sidetracked by high energy in body, go for a jog; feel focused, do extra work to capitalize on being "in the zone."
Energy Regulation	The ability to maintain an energy level that is a match for the activity at hand (e.g., high energy for football game; medium energy when taking a test; low energy to fall asleep).	Feel high energy (antsy) during class, seek quick walk to water fountain; feel low energy (tired) during homework, seek a cold drink.
Emotion Regulation	This is the ability to monitor and control emotions.	Feel slightly frustrated, seek help; feel overwhelmed, take a deep breath; feel sad, seek comfort from family.

Note: Most subtypes of self-regulation overlap and are interdependent processes. However, especially when planning a comprehensive intervention plan, it is helpful to view different aspects of self-regulation in a separate manner to ensure all aspects involved with self-regulation are addressed.

Self-Regulation and Body States

The ability to detect body states is vital to our health, well-being and even survival. Interoception plays a critical role in our ability to regulate our body functions. We rely on information from the interoceptive system to alert us to the need for action. For example, a clear signal from our bladder can alert us that it is full and we need to act. Or a clear signal from an area of injury can alert us that it is very painful and we need to act.

Interoception and body states are inseparable. That is, we rely on awareness of our interoceptive signals, or IA, to detect our body state. Given that our body state provides us with crucial information regarding many bodily functions, without good IA we would not be able regulate our most basic body functions. This can lead to issues related to quality of life, health and independent living.

Self-Regulation and Emotion States

Emotion states (hereafter simply referred to as emotions) are an essential part of the human experience. Some of the most prominent theories on emotions propose that emotions arise directly from our internal body signals (Craig, 2002, 2009; Damasio, 1994, 1996; James, 1884). That is, in order for an emotional experience to occur, changes within our body have to occur. For example, it is not possible to feel afraid without sensing muscle trembling or tension, a fast heart rate, fluttery stomach or shortness of breath.

Interoception and emotions cannot be separated. That is, our internal body signals are essential to our emotional experience. In fact, interoception is so closely linked to our emotional experience that it is reflected in our everyday language (Lakoff & Johnson, 1980). For example, consider the phrases we might use to describe nervousness – cold feet, butterflies in stomach – or the phrase "broken-hearted" to describe emotional hurt. All of these use a body sensation to express an emotion.

Extensive, brain-based evidence has revealed the connection between interoception and emotion. In fact, the insula – the interoception center of the brain – is activated during virtually every brain imaging study on human emotions ever done (Craig, 2003). In other words, the insula shows activity during tasks designed to evoke emotion. In a split second, the internal sensations from our organs and tissues are sent to the brain (mainly the insula) and the insula uses these sensations to figure out the current emotion.

"Feeling" an Emotion

Good IA allows us to clearly *feel* emotions in the body (Craig, 2002, 2014; Critchley et al., 2004; Herbert, Herbert, & Pollatos, 2011; Herbert, Pollatos, & Schandry, 2007; Lane, Sechrest, Riedel, Shapiro, & Kaszniak, 2000; Pollatos, Gramann, & Schandry, 2007; Pollatos et al., 2005). Emotions can arise by localized, distinct sensations or from more global, general sensations. For example, sadness may be felt locally as a lump in the throat, a tightening in the chest or belly, *or* more globally as a painful wave spreading through the entire body (Fuchs & Koch, 2014). These body sensations vary depending on the emotion. Sadness feels different from nervousness. Calmness feels different from embarrassment. Furthermore, they vary depending on the degree or

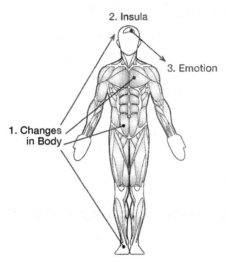

intensity within one emotion. A little happy feels different from really, really happy. A little angry feels different from really, really angry.

The ability to differentiate our body sensations and make sense of them allows us to differentiate between emotions (Füstos, Gramann, Herbert, & Pollatos, 2012). Therefore, the ability to distinguish or feel subtle differences between them via our interoceptive system is crucial to the emotional experience. In a large study, Herbert et al. (2011) found that the participants who scored better on a measure of interoception were also far better at understanding their own distinct emotions, thus revealing that **good IA leads to good emotional awareness.**

"Feeling" Different Emotions

The ability to identify distinct emotions comes into play constantly throughout the course of a day. Even in a single situation, we can experience a range of emotions (Demiralp et al., 2012). Imagine you are about to meet a blind date for dinner. You might be filled with *excitement* over a new adventure. You might also feel *nervous* about meeting a new person. Maybe you are a bit *worried* that you might not have much in common with your date and that the dinner could be awkward. You might also feel *thankful* because your friend set you up with this date. Perhaps you feel a bit *frustrated* because your last date did not turn out as you had hoped, but you feel *determined* to keep trying to find that perfect match.

Key Point

Good Emotional Awareness	Poor Emotional Awareness
People with good emotion awareness are thought to have a well-working interoceptive system. They receive clear body signals, which allow them to detect differences in the way each emotion feels. This leads them to determining the fine differences between emotions. Due to their ability to identify their emotions with high levels of clarity, people with good emotion awareness are also better at controlling their emotions.	People with poor emotional awareness can have an ineffective interoceptive system that does not provide clear body signals. Without the clear body signals, they do not notice subtle differences in the way each emotion feels and in turn have difficulty identifying their emotions, especially the subtle or less intense emotions. This reduced ability to identify emotions creates a challenge for people with poor emotion awareness to control their emotions.

As in the situation above, most people experience distinct, highly specific emotions and are effortlessly aware of each discrete emotion. To do this, we rely a great deal on how each emotion "feels" in the body.

Emotional awareness varies between individuals. Some people have good emotional awareness and can easily feel each distinct emotion, as in the first-date example above. Others have poor emotional awareness and are not able to determine various emotions with great clarity. They might report a general feeling of good or bad, but not be able to discriminate any further. Or they might detect a basic emotion, like anger, but can't determine the intensity (i.e., a little angry vs. exploding angry). Or, as in the first date example, they might recognize a general feeling of excitement but miss the other emotions intermingled with the excitement.

Importance of "Feeling" Different Emotions

The ability to distinguish between emotions has far-reaching benefits. Researchers have been interested in the impact emotion differentiation, or lack thereof, can have on a variety of areas. Several of these findings are summarized in Table 1.4.

Table 1.4

Good vs. Poor Emotional Awareness

Good Emotional Awareness	Poor Emotional Awareness
Better able to adapt to events and "go with the flow"	Often rigid and inflexible; like things to be the same
Good control of emotions	Lack of good control of emotions
A larger repertoire of healthy, effective coping skills	Limited repertoire of effective coping skills; sometimes unhealthy coping strategies are employed (e.g., self-injury, substance abuse)
Less aggressive behaviors when experiencing anger	Less control over emotions results in higher occurrence of intense emotions and related behaviors (e.g., meltdowns, aggression)
Less maladaptive coping mechanisms such as alcohol abuse	Limited repertoire of effective coping skills can lead to desperate attempts to find other methods of coping such as alcohol abuse
Lower rates of depression	High rates of depression
Good self-esteem	Low self-esteem
Good ability to read others' emotions	Difficulty reading others' emotions
Able to "feel" others' emotions; good empathy	Reduced ability to "feel" others' emotions; poor empathy

Adapted from Barrett, Gross, Christenson, & Benvenuto (2001); Demiralp et al. (2012); Erbas, Ceulemans, Boonen, Noens, & Kuppens (2013); Erbas, Ceulemans, Lee Pe, Koval, & Kuppens (2014); Kashdan & Farmer (2014); Kashdan, Ferssizidis, Collins, & Muraven (2010); Pond, Kashdan, DeWall, Savostyanova, Lambert, & Fincham (2012); and Tugade, Fredrickson, & Feldman Barrett (2004).

Emotional Regulation

Effective IA leads to the fine-tuned understanding of emotions. It is this fine-tuned understanding of emotions that is a key foundation for emotional regulation (Barrett et al., 2001; Gross, 1998). Very simply speaking, *emotional regulation* refers to the processes by which we control our emotions.

Although we control both positive and negative emotions, typically the greatest press for emotion regulation comes when we are faced with intense negative emotions such as anger, fear and sadness (Barrett et al., 2001). We need to be able to quickly regain our balance (homeostasis) when faced with a distressing situation. Distinctly feeling a negative emotion provides valuable information about the situation at hand (e.g., that it is aversive) and signals the need to take action (Füstos et al., 2012).

Typically, the action we take to regulate our emotions falls into one or both of the following categories.

1. **We use a strategy that directly alters the current emotion.**
   During a recent math class, MJ could not find her favorite pencil, and she began to feel her muscles tense, her heart rate slightly increase and a general feeling of warmth overspread her body. She knew this meant she was growing frustrated. MJ asked to take a quick walk to reduce her feelings of frustration. When she returned she removed her stress ball from her desk and squeezed it a few times. The walk and stress ball helped to alter the current emotion, and she was feeling calm once again. Given that she could think more rationally when she was calm, MJ decided it wasn't a big deal if she had to use her second favorite pencil to complete her math work.

2. **We use a strategy that alters the current situation.**
   During a recent math class, MJ could not find her favorite pencil, and she began to feel her muscles tense, her heart rate slightly increase and a general feeling of warmth overspread her body. She knew this meant she was growing frustrated. She decided to ask the teacher for help finding her pencil. Together they searched her desk and could not find it. The teacher offered to share one of her special pencils with MJ. All of the students loved using one of the teacher's special pencils, so this pleased MJ greatly. Asking the teacher for help altered the current situation that was causing her frustration. Together, MJ and the teacher found a solution and MJ was able to move on and complete her math work using a different pencil.

In both scenarios, MJ was attempting to control the emotion. We do this kind of thing all day long, whether it is to increase, decrease or maintain an emotion (Mazefsky, Borue, Day, & Minshew, 2014). That is, we continually attempt to maintain our internal balance.

Successful employment of effective emotional regulation strategies requires good insight into our current emotional state (Lambie & Marcel, 2002). We need to know what we are feeling so we know what to do about it. For that, we rely on interoception for clear information about our emotions. **In other words, good IA leads to good emotional regulation** (Füstos et al., 2012).

Individuals with poor IA lack insight into their emotions and have limited information alerting them with the urge to act or the urge to use emotional regulation strategies. Not surprisingly, therefore, they often experience emotional regulation difficulties, including experiencing meltdowns, high anxiety, rigid and inflexible thinking, overwhelming emotions and reactions, resistance to change and poor problem solving.

Problem Solving

As in the case of MJ above, interoception acts as first line of defense when we are faced with a potential problem. That is, our body warns us of a problem, and we begin working towards the most advantageous outcome. Therefore, good IA significantly increases the likelihood of being able to quickly recognize and solve a problem (Lane & Schwartz, 1987).

Learning About the World

In addition to our internal needs, interoception helps us learn about our external surroundings. From birth, we are bombarded by experiences, and over time we start to notice how certain experiences make us feel internally. That is, we take note of the body signals evoked during each experience and use them to determine the quality of the experience. Does the experience make us feel good or does it make us feel bad? Gradually, we begin to fine-tune this process and begin to naturally link a particular collection of body signals to a specific emotion. For example, when we feel our muscles shake, our heart race and our stomach quiver, we start to realize that this means we are nervous. We then use this information to determine the quality of a situation with emotional detail. Did an experience make us feel comfortable or happy, or did it make us feel upset or terrified? As we grow, we develop connections between a given experience, the body sensations evoked and the corresponding emotion, and store our observations for later use. The well-known neuroscientist Antonio Damasio (1994) calls these stored observations **somatic markers**.

In his famous somatic marker theory, Damasio (1994) explains that in order to make the brain work as efficiently as possible, the somatic markers form a built-in prediction system that makes educated guesses based on past experience. That is, when we encounter an object, person, place or experience, our brain retrieves the past information and helps us make predictions about the present. In other words, we call on the corresponding somatic marker to tell us how the current object, person, place

Interoception as Our Body's Emotion Gauge

How do you know when you need to stop for gas? You rely on your car's gasoline gauge to let you know the current gasoline level in you car. Based on the signal it sends you, you know exactly what action you need to take: If it is close to full, you can keep on going without worry. If it is in the middle, you can keep going, but should make a plan to stop for gas sometime in the next 100 miles. If you are near empty, you know you need to take action to fill the tank and get the gauge back near full.

Now imagine if your gasoline gauge stopped working. Without clear, specific information, it would be challenging to discern the exact level of gasoline in your tank. You might call on logic to calculate approximately how much gas you have in the tank – maybe you try to figure out how many days it has been since you filled up with gas or try to calculate how many miles you've traveled since your last refill. Such a logical process might get you close, but without the well-defined, reliable signals from the gauge you cannot determine exactly how full the tank is. As a result, you have a much higher chance of finding yourself out of gas, car sputtering and leaving you stranded, miles away from a gas station.

Your interoceptive system serves as your body's invisible gasoline gauge. Interoception provides you with clear information about the various levels within your body – how hungry or full you feel; how tired or energized you feel; how stressed or relaxed you feel; and so on. Based on the signal your interoceptive system sends, you know exactly what action you need to take.

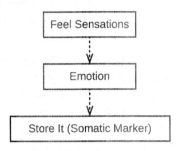

Good IA allows the body to continually sense what is in the environment and interpret how it makes us feel. This process feeds the formation of somatic markers.

or experience makes us feel. Is it safe? Does it make us feel good? Does it make us feel nervous? In turn, we use that information to make a speedy decision, whether to approach, avoid, persist, walk away and so on. It happens in a blink of an eye and requires little to no thought or effort.

Decision Making and Intuition

The Two Sides of Decision Making: One leads with the heart
(emotion) and one leads with the brain (logic)

In the past, making decisions was regarded as a rational, cognitive process in which we think through a situation, analyzing the choices and related outcomes. However, more recent approaches incorporate the idea that interoceptive signals, emotions and somatic markers play an important role in decision making (Bechara, Damasio, Tranel, & Damasio, 1997; Gu, Wang, et al., 2015; Xiang, Lohrenz, & Montague, 2013).

Through the formation of somatic markers, we have a speedy system in place that alerts us to positive and negative aspects of a situation and allows for thought-free, intuitive decision making (Dunn et al., 2010; Werner, Jung, Duschek, & Schandry, 2009). **The interoceptive signals form our so-called gut feelings and help us to "follow our gut," so to speak, rather than think through the situation.** Therefore, awareness of these interoceptive signals (or IA) becomes an essential part of an intuitive, "gut-driven," decision-making process (Damasio, 1996; Gu, Hof, et al., 2013; Gu, Wang, et al., 2015; Gu & Fitzgerald, 2014).

Key Point

A quick review: Somatic markers contain information about a specific situation and the feelings it evoked in the past. Did this situation ... make us feel good? Feel bad? Feel scared? Feel comfortable?

New views on human behavior suggest that it can be guided by decisions rooted in a speedy, emotion-driven process (i.e., intuitive – following your gut – not-thinking-through-it decision), *or* a slower, logical cognitive process (i.e., analyzing the situation – weighing-my-options-carefully decision), *or* a combination of the two (Evans, 2003).

Both processes have their advantages (see Table 1.5). The emotion-driven process is faster, can handle far more information at once and intuitively takes into account the context of the situation. But it is less accurate. The cognitive process, on the other hand, is more deliberate and much less efficient, requiring more energy, but it can lead to more favorable results (De Martino, Harrison, Knafo, Bird, & Dolan, 2008; Kahneman, 2003).

Individuals with poor IA have difficulty using the intuitive, emotional process and instead tend to rely on the rational, logical thinking process to guide their decisions. The resulting rule-bound, logical, concrete system can be slow and exhausting, especially in the face of new or unpredictable situations. The result may be a desire for sameness, reduced flexibility, difficulty adapting in uncertain environments and an inability to keep pace with rapidly changing social contexts (De Martino et al., 2008).

Table 1.5
The Two Sides of Decision Making

Emotion-Driven Decision Making	Cognitive Decision Making
Intuitive	Logical
Fast	Deliberate
Effortless	Controlled
Automatic	Rule Governed
Guided by learning from past experiences	Effortful
	Hypothetical (what could happen)
Based on DeMartino et al. (2008), Evans (2003), and Kahneman (2003).	

The Science Behind "Gut Feelings"

Bechara and Damasio (2005) used the well-known Iowa Gambling Task to show just how powerful a role our interoceptive signals, or gut feelings, play in the decision-making process. Bechara, Damasio, Tranel, & Damasio (2005) asked participants in their study to play a simple card game. Each person received four decks of cards and a sum of money.

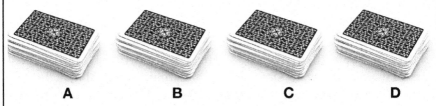

A   **B**   **C**   **D**

Participants were instructed to flip cards from any of the four decks, one-by-one, while trying to lose the least amount of money and win the most. What they were not told was that decks A and B were risky; they had huge dollar rewards but also huge penalties. Conversely, decks C and D offered small rewards but also small penalties. In fact, the only way a person could win was by sticking to decks C and D, earning a small but more consistent payout.

The researchers were interested in how long it would take for participants to figure out which decks were the "good decks" and which were the "bad decks." What they found was that it took participants about fifty cards to develop a hunch about the decks. They didn't know *why* they preferred decks C and D but were fairly certain that they were better choices. By card eighty, most had figured out the task and were able to clearly explain why decks A and B were "bad" and C and D were "good."

What made this task the most interesting was that participants were hooked up to a device that measured the amount of sweat moisture on their skin. This is because our sweat glands respond to stress (think clammy hands), and the researchers were interested in determining the point during the task at which the participants began developing a stress response. Here is what they found: Participants developed a stress response in anticipation of selecting a card from the "bad decks" by the tenth card: forty cards before they developed a conscious hunch *and* seventy cards before they could consciously and clearly explain the task.

Interestingly, right around the tenth card, the same time that the stress response was noted to start, the participants' behaviors began to change. They unknowingly started to favor the "good decks" even before developing a conscious hunch. This means that they had figured out the task before they knew they had figured out the task: they were making decisions before they were consciously aware of what decisions they should be making (Gladwell, 2007). In other words, they started to use their gut to make decisions long before they started using logical thinking. Interoceptive signals were far faster than logical thinking.

Flexibility of Thought

Quick decision making and the ability to think flexibly go hand in hand. Intuitive, emotion-driven decision making enables us to react quickly in situations that otherwise involve a high degree of uncertainty. Frequently, when determining the appropriate course of action, we do not have time to perform careful analyses via our logic-driven decision system. Instead, we must rely on these rapid intuitive judgments assisted by our past experiences and somatic markers. The formation of these intuitive somatic markers is dependent on the pairing of clear interoceptive signals and emotions. Thus, interoception becomes an important foundation of our intuition, our ability to judge situations quickly and accurately, our ability to sense risk and reward and our ability to analyze and adapt to rapidly changing conditions. **In other words, with good IA, we are able to behave or act more flexibly. It allows us to "go with the flow."**

Social Awareness and the Hidden Curriculum

Consider the complexity of each social situation you encounter – think about the unpredictable nature and how the context is constantly changing. No two social situations are the same. Our insula is a main contributor to helping us intuitively navigate these social moments using our emotion-driven decision systems. Over time, through the formation of somatic markers, interoception provides the foundation for us to naturally "know" what is expected in a given situation. We don't often have to think about what to do; we just naturally do it. With little effort, we continually assess the situation, adapt to changes, keep the rhythm with those around us and persist through challenging moments. How difficult would it be if we lacked this intuition, these gut feelings, this natural ability to "just know what to do"? Without this speedy, innate process to help us through each situation, social situations would become challenging and exhausting, to say the least.

This natural ability to "know" what to do in individual social situations allows us to stay in line with the social norms or expectations of each situation. We can naturally adapt our actions or behavior to ever-changing expectations. Over time, our interoceptive system allows us to develop an intuitive base of knowledge regarding social norms, those unwritten rules that we instinctively learn, also referred to as the "hidden curriculum" (Myles, Endow, & Mayfield, 2013; Myles & Kolar, 2013; Myles, Trautman, & Schelvan, 2013).

This knowledge of the hidden curriculum helps us to get by socially without the need to think through the situation. The rules become instincts that we can automatically call on or act on without much thought. Without this base of knowledge regarding the hidden curriculum, navigating social situations would be difficult. Unintentional social mistakes and norm violations would likely occur regularly.

Perspective Taking and Empathy

In addition to its strong role in the above areas, interoception also has responsibilities in social cognitive areas such as perspective taking and empathy (Craig, 2009; Grynberg & Pollatos, 2015; Lamm & Singer, 2010; Silani, Bird, Brindley, Singer, Frith, & Frith, 2008; Singer, Seymour, O'Doherty, Kaube, Dolan, & Frith, 2004). Remember Damasio's (1994) somatic marker hypothesis? Not only do these markers allow us to predict our own reaction to events, they also allow us to predict how others may think and feel in the same or similar circumstance.

We can infer the interoceptive signals another might experience based on what interoceptive signals we have experienced in the past. In other words, we understand other people's feelings based on simulating how we might feel in a given situation. As such, interoception allows us to "put ourselves in someone else's shoes." **Interoception not only allows us to answer the question "How do *I* feel?," it allows us to answer the question, "How do *you* feel?"**

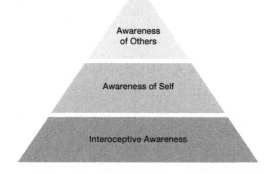

Good IA provides a foundation for self-awareness. This clear sense of self is necessary before developing a clear sense of others.

An intriguing study by Singer and colleagues (2004) used imaging technology to measure the brain activity of their participants when receiving a painful stimulus. The researchers then measured participants' brain activity while watching a loved one receiving the same painful stimuli. The researchers found that the insula was activated *both* when the participants received pain *and* when they witnessed a loved one receiving pain. Therefore, both the first-hand experience of pain and the second-hand experience of seeing another person experiencing pain activated the insula in the same manner. This provides evidence that empathy is in part rooted in using our own experience of the interoceptive signals evoked by a given situation to understand the interoceptive signals of another. That is, **we infer the interoceptive signals and emotions of others based on our own interoceptive signals and emotions.**

Additional research has demonstrated similar insula activation during other negative and positive emotions, such as disgust, anger and happiness (Gu, Hof, et al., 2013; Singer, et al., 2004). Taken together, these findings show that the insula, and thus interoception, plays a role in both feeling our own emotions and "feeling" the emotions of other people (Lamm & Singer, 2010).

Notably, aspects of social cognition such as perspective taking and empathy not only require us to *think* about the contents of someone else's mind, they also include the ability to *feel* someone else's emotions and experiences. Research has shown that this ability to "feel" someone else's emotions is correlated with our ability to feel our own emotions (Silani, et al., 2008). In other words, **people who are good at feeling their own emotions are usually good at feeling the emotions of others ... and the key factor to "feeling" our own emotions? Interoception!**

Social Touch

Recent research has discovered that our interoceptive sense plays an important role in how we experience touch. The sense of touch has a well-known main branch that helps us to manipulate and explore objects and provides us information about physical qualities (e.g., shape, weight, texture). However, the sense of touch also has a distinct second branch that is involved in the social aspects of touch (McGlone, Wessberg, & Olausson, 2014; Olausson, Wessberg, McGlone, & Vallbo, 2010).

Slow, gentle touch on certain areas of the body, those areas that are covered in fine hair (e.g., the arm, but not the palm of the hand), activates a special type of touch receptor called C tactile fibers or CT fibers for short (McGlone, et al., 2014; Olausson, et al., 2010). When the CT fibers are stimulated by gentle, light touch, a signal travels a pathway to the insula (Olausson, et al., 2002), making it a crucial part of our interoceptive system and thus providing us with the emotional and social side of touch. Therefore, with the help of the CT fibers, our interoceptive system plays a vital role in the experience of touch as an important aspect of social interaction and emotional well-being. For example, light touch allows for the formation of social bonds between a parent and child, trusted friendships, and romantic relationships. Social touch can elicit reassuring, pleasant feelings, thus creating an experience that is rewarding and motivating.

Awareness of Self

As we have seen, interoception is a key player in many different areas. However, perhaps most important, interoception provides us with a basic sense of self (Craig, 2009; Damasio, 2010) and ownership of our own body (Herbert & Pollatos, 2012; Tsakiris, Hesse, Boy, Haggard, & Fink, 2007). In other words, **interoception gives us the sense that "this is me; this is my body; this is how I feel."**

Brain research reveals that the insula, the interoceptive center in the brain, is active during self-reflection (Modinos, Ormel, & Aleman, 2009) as well as when we look at our own reflection in the mirror and look at a picture of ourselves, thus providing evidence that interoception is involved in these important aspects of self-awareness. Conversely, individuals with insula damage have been shown to be unaware of their bodies, to lack the ability to self-reflect and recognize themselves in a mirror, further supporting the connection between interoception and a sense of self.

The sense of self enables us to reflect upon ourselves, allowing for introspection and thus assessment of our behavior in relation to the world and others around us. So not only are interoception and self-awareness important to our ability to control our body (e.g., self-regulation) (Paulus & Stein, 2010), they also form a social foundation for how we behave and interact with our surroundings (Seth, 2013).

Self-awareness allows for development of a first-person perspective, providing us with a connection to our own thoughts, feelings, intentions and body. Once our self-perspective is solid, it provides us with a foundation for understanding the thoughts, feelings, intentions and bodies of those around us. Therefore, **good IA is essential to our core human experience, providing us with a clear sense of self and others** (Craig, 2014).

Summary

As illustrated, a well-functioning interoceptive system contributes to the successful performance of many vital skills. So what happens when the interoceptive system is not functioning at an optimal level? In an effort to answer this question, researchers have studied the cases of individuals who have either experienced a change of or sustained an injury to the insula. For example, significant insula degeneration occurs in individuals with a disease known as frontotemporal dementia. Due to the changes in the insula, these individuals experience some of the following symptoms:

- loss of perspective taking and the ability to identify how someone else might be feeling (empathy)

- loss of social tact

- decreased ability to assess risk

- decreased awareness of social norms

- diminished self-control (at times overeating or substance abuse)

- difficulty controlling emotions and corresponding behaviors

Although much has been discovered in the past decade or two, researchers have still not been able to determine why some people are born with insula that never seem to reach an optimal level of functioning. Decreased insula functioning has been correlated with a variety of diagnoses, including eating disorders, ADHD, obsessive-compulsive disorder, post-traumatic stress disorder, bipolar disorder, depression, anxiety, schizophrenia, substance abuse and ASD. In Chapter 2, we will look at the specific connection between the insula, interoception and ASD.

CHAPTER 2

Interoception and Autism

Sensory issues are highly prevalent among individuals with ASD (see Myles et al., 2014, for full review). In fact, sensory difficulties are so common – rates among individuals with ASD may be as high as 95% (Baker, Lane, Angley, & Young, 2008; Baranek, David, Poe, Stone, & Watson, 2006; Dunn, Myles, & Orr, 2002; Tomchek & Dunn, 2007) – that they are now included as a diagnostic criterion for ASD in the *Diagnostic and Statistical Manual of Mental Disorders, 5*[th] *Edition* (DSM-5; American Psychiatric Association, 2013).

Sensory issues vary greatly between individuals and even within the same person (see Myles et al., 2014, for full review). They can impact one sensory system or multiple sensory systems. Some people are overresponsive to sensations, which means they respond rapidly to sensory input. These individuals find certain sensations to be intense, uncomfortable and even painful. Other people are underresponsive to sensory input, which can make them slow to respond. These individuals may miss sensory information entirely or need a large dose of sensory input in order to notice or respond.

Many individuals with ASD also have difficulties with their eighth sensory system – interoception. However, interoception is not yet well known or well researched in the autism field, so many people do not realize or attribute the experienced difficulties to poor interoceptive awareness (see Tables 2.1, 2.2 and 2.3 for examples).

As information about interoception is spreading, individuals with ASD are starting to share personal accounts regarding their experience with interoception-related challenges. Chloe, a 22-year-old woman with ASD, shares the following:

I did not realize I had trouble feeling my internal body signals, as I had never heard of interoception before November 2014, but when I did, everything started to make sense. That is, difficulties with interoception help to explain why I have such a hard time explaining when I am not feeling well, why sometimes I seem to eat snack after snack without feeling full and why I get upset/anxious/overwhelmed so quickly, because I don't feel it until I'm already far into the storm of the discomfort and frustration.

It has helped me to learn about interoception. It has given me a name for it and allowed me to think and realize that it was something I struggled with. After learning about interoception at a conference, I was encouraged and motivated to find an occupational therapist to work on "feeling" my body better. Going to occupational therapy is one of the best decisions I've made. All around I've been impacted positively.

I'm still new on this journey with interoception, but I have started to label more how my body may be feeling when I don't feel well. "My throat feels inflamed." "It feels like something is pushing on my stomach." Phrases that before I was overall not able to use, everything "just hurt," or "hurt, yes, no, maybe" or crying and screaming over it hurting and wanting it fixed ASAP. Some of this is still an issue, and I am not able to consistently communicate hurt and discomfort, but I've definitely had some positive gains! I've also started to feel emotions and communicate them. Recently I did this in a high-anxiety situation, I was able to text my therapist while sitting next to her at a meeting, "All done. I don't like this. I feel frustrated. I feel overwhelmed." This is not something that I would have likely done before. Usually my first response would be screaming or crying or getting frustrated. Instead, even when my brain was feeling stuck and anxious, I was able to communicate that I was feeling very overwhelmed and frustrated. My therapist was then able to suggest taking a walk, and I took a break and got deep pressure. I calmed down quicker and did not have a total meltdown in the situation; instead, I communicated that I needed to leave in an acceptable manner, and with support, I was able to regulate again.

I want others to know that interoception, like all other sensory differences are REAL. It is hard, not knowing exactly how your body feels.

Chloe's report illustrates the important role that interoception plays as well as the significant impact that reduced IA can have.

Fiene and Brownlow (2015) looked at the interoceptive experiences of people with ASD; specifically, 74 adults diagnosed with ASD and 228 adults without ASD. They found that participants in the ASD group reported significantly lower IA. This is the first research article to date showing that interoceptive difficulties do indeed warrant further attention and may be behind many of the challenges experienced by people with ASD.

Interoception, the Brain and Autism

While Fiene and Barlow (2015) were the first to directly look at interoception in individuals with ASD, numerous studies have examined the insula, or the brain's interoception center, in people with ASD. These studies, some of which are summarized below, show a significant difference between the insula in individuals with ASD and those without ASD.

- **Connectivity both within subdivisions of the insula and between the insula and other areas of the brain** – In a large study, data collected from 539 adolescents and adults with ASD and 573 age-matched typical controls demonstrated a hypo-connectivity (hypo meaning "too low") of the mid and posterior insula in autism (Di Martino et al., 2014).

  In contrast, one of the first brain imaging studies of the insula of young children with ASD (ages 7-12 years old) found a hyper-connectivity (hyper meaning "too high") of the insula (Uddin, Supekar, Lynch, et al., 2013). This finding suggests that at some point a shift may occur from the hyper-connectivity seen in younger children to the hypo-connectivity found in adolescents and adults. As a result, developmental changes in functional connectivity in the insula might be one hallmark of ASD (Dickstein et al., 2013; Nomi & Uddin, 2015).

- **Activity within the insula** – Across 24 studies that imaged the brains of individuals with ASD, the insula was consistently found to demonstrate decreased activity when compared to people without ASD (Di Martino, Ross, Uddin, Sklar, & Costellanos, 2009).

- **Structural differences** – Radeloff et al. (2014) found that people with ASD when compared to typically developing control subjects showed reduced gray matter volume in the insula.

Taken together, the emerging picture is that functional connectivity patterns, level of activity and the structure of the insula are impacted in many people with ASD. Given that the insula is the interoception center in the brain, this provides a brain-based explanation for the interoceptive difficulties reported by many individuals with ASD and sheds light on many of the often mysterious characteristics of ASD.

Reduced Interoceptive Awareness

Personal accounts, brain studies and other research have made it increasingly clear that poor IA is common in many, but not all, individuals with ASD. Reduced IA makes it difficult to answer questions such as, "How do you feel?," "How does your body feel when you are angry?," "How does your body feel when you are calm?" or "Do you feel thirsty?"

The challenges with interoception and IA fall into three main categories (for more information, see Myles, et al., 2014): interoceptive overresponsivity, interoceptive underresponsivity and interoceptive discrimination difficulty.

Interoceptive Overresponsivity

Individuals who have interoceptive overresponsivity may feel their internal states more readily. In fact, many times, they "over-feel" these internal sensations, causing them to be distracted by or highly anxious over them. These individuals may feel a lot of sensations all at once, which can be very overwhelming and confusing. Livi, a 10-year-old girl with ASD, explained it well, "It just feels so noisy inside my body. I'm not sure what it all means."

Due to the overresponsivity, some individuals with ASD feel so many different internal signals at once that they have trouble discerning which clues are salient, or important, and therefore require attention. Due to the "noisy" nature of the overresponsivity, the signals are unclear and inconclusive, thus resulting in poor IA.

*When **Gertie, a 13-year-old girl with ASD,** was asked to complete a stress thermometer at school, she was able to label each of the 10 degrees of stress very well (0 being calm and 10 being the extremely stressed). She was then asked to fill in a side column that described what her body felt like at each level. Gertie was able to do this in great detail, including a minimum of nine body symptoms for each of the degrees. In fact, she included so many details that she had to expand her thermometer to be twice as long as the rest of her classmates. Her teachers were very excited but also confused.*

They were puzzled by the fact that Gertie could report such detail for each degree of stress. Apparently, she was feeling changes in her stress levels, yet she was still having major self-regulation difficulties, including daily meltdowns and frequent refusals to leave the learning support classroom. Through discussion with Gertie, it was discovered that yes, she was feeling her interoceptive signals, but it was too much. During stressful moments, she was bombarded and overcome by all of the internal sensations. This internal noise caused an even higher level of anxiety. Although Gertie could feel many different internal sensations, her overresponsivity led to poor IA.

Interoceptive Underresponsivity

As opposed to overresponsivity, individuals who experience interoceptive underresponsivity may not notice their internal body signals unless they are extremely intense. Often individuals in this category do not feel building body states or emotions and do not identify a body state or emotion until it is very intense (see Table 2.2). The reduced ability to feel their internal signals leads to poor IA.

Table 2.1
Interoceptive Overresponsivity and Body States

What You Might Observe	Relation to Poor IA
The child requests bathroom breaks very frequently.	The child is extra sensitive to the urge to urinate or eliminate bowels. The slightest urge causes a feeling of discomfort or emergency.
The child visits the nurse's office several times a week complaining of aches, pains and ailments.	The child overly feels internal states and the slightest discomfort can feel like a major health issue.
The child limps on an injured ankle for weeks longer than expected.	The child continues to feel pain in the ankle even when it might seem slight or almost healed to others.

Table 2.1 (*continued*)

Interoceptive Overresponsivity and Emotions

What You Might Observe	Relation to Poor IA
During the winter, the child refuses to take jacket off when coming in from recess.	The child's awareness of body temperature is keen and they feel colder much longer than the other students. It takes them much longer to "feel" warm.
The child seems always to be hungry and/or thirsty.	The child might feel hunger or thirst much quicker when compared to the other students. The smallest twinge of hunger or thirst may feel very intense, like not having eaten or drunk water in days.
The child seems to panic after a short period of physical exertion.	The child may be very sensitive to the increase in heart rate and/or breathing. These feelings can be uncomfortable and/or intense, causing him to panic.
The child is overly dramatic when she has a seemingly minor ailment (e.g., hangnail, runny nose or stubbed toe).	To a child who is highly sensitive to her internal body states like pain, the feeling is amplified significantly.
When in a calm state, the child is able to identify a seemingly endless list of internal signals linked to a given emotion only to be unable to identify it when experiencing it in the moment.	In the heat of the moment, the child is so sensitive to the internal signals that he feels too many signals at once. This can be overwhelming and make it difficult to know which signals are most important for navigating situations.
The child reports feeling so many internal signals that it is "noisy."	The child is very sensitive to every internal signal, creating a feeling of internal chaos.
The child reports feeling many different internal sensations but is unable to determine the current emotion.	The signals are too overwhelming and unclear, resulting in an inability to select the most relevant signals to determine the emotion.

When **Jaquan, a 25-year-old young man with ASD**, started OT, he reported the following: *"I do not realize that I am getting angry until I am* *exploding with anger. By then it is too late. The feelings are overwhelming. I have little control." Jaquan was missing the early signals of his building anger and never noticed the subtle changes associated with emotions such as irritation, annoyance and frustration. For Jaquan, his emotions were black and white. He either felt calm or "exploding with anger," which caused him to miss opportunities to use self-regulation strategies before it was too late.*

Due to reduced ability to feel the internal body signals, often people with interoceptive underresponsivity use logical methods to figure out their emotions, but that can be very inefficient and unreliable.

__Declan, a 14-year-old with ASD__, shared the following about his experience before improving his IA: "I felt nothing in my body. I found it strange when my OT asked me what my body felt like when I was angry or when I was excited. I just didn't feel my body change at all. And I didn't realize that other people felt their emotions that way. In the past, I would sometimes figure out how I was feeling by my actions. Like after I hit or punched something, I knew I must be angry."

__Hollis, an 18-year-old with ASD__, reported similar experiences, as he did not realize how he was feeling through interoception. Rather, he would have to logically figure out how he was feeling based on his or others' actions. For example, when he first realized that he liked a girl, it was not through butterflies in his stomach. He logically concluded that he liked her because he was thinking about her a lot. Hollis used a logical assessment of emotions, not a sensation-driven process.

Interoceptive Discrimination Difficulty

Individuals who have interoceptive discrimination difficulty cannot always pinpoint the exact feeling they sense internally. They might have a vague or general feeling but have difficulty identifying exactly what the sensation means (see Table 2.3).

__Frank, an 8-year-old with ASD__, reported that he was angry whenever he felt any type of discomfort in his body. When he was nervous, he reported anger. When he was annoyed, anger. When he was hungry, anger. When he had to go to the bathroom, anger. He was able to feel a vague sense of discomfort but could not differentiate the sensations.

Table 2.2
Interoceptive Underresponsivity and Body States

What You Might Observe	Relation to Poor IA
When needing to eliminate waste, the child seems to always wait until the last minute and then races to the bathroom.	The child does not effectively process signals from the bladder and/or intestinal tract and does not sense the need to use the bathroom until the feeling is very extreme.
The child is difficult to toilet train, having frequent accidents and never telling the adult that he needs to use the bathroom.	The child does not sense the urge to eliminate waste and therefore never tells an adult that he needs to use the bathroom.
The child never seems to feel hungry and/or thirsty and almost needs to be "forced" to eat or drink.	The child does not effectively process the signals regarding hunger and thirst and simply does not feel the discomfort.
The child may have a fairly significant health issue and never complain of symptoms (e.g., strep throat, urinary tract infection, broken finger, fever).	The child does not sense the discomfort in her throat, urinary tract or finger and therefore does not report it.
The child keeps running until she reaches a point of extreme exhaustion.	During physical exertion, the child does not sense the signals of "too much" activity and therefore does not stop or take a break.

Interoceptive Underresponsivity and Emotions

What You Might Observe	Relation to Poor IA
The child has difficulty recognizing the early signs of an emotion and seems to have "all-or-none" emotions.	The child does not sense the subtle changes in his body such as faster heart and breathing rate and tense muscles. He only senses these changes when they are at the extreme.
The child has difficulty using calming strategies effectively; once she senses stress, it is often too late.	Once a child's stress/emotions are intense, it is often too late to use a calming strategy effectively. The key is to use the strategy at the start of the stress, when it is less intense. The child does not sense her body signals of early stress and therefore does not recognize the need for the calming strategies.
When asked how his body feels during certain emotions, the child is unable to answer with clarity.	The child does not feel the subtle changes in his body and may not recognize a variety of emotions because he has never "felt" them before.

Carmen, a 10-year-old girl with ASD, also experienced vague sensations and often could not make fine-tuned guesses about her body states and emotions. She reported the following, "I can feel strange feelings in this area [pointing to her abdomen], but I have no idea what it means. Sometimes, I think, 'maybe I'm hungry,' so I get food, but then can't eat it, so I don't think it is hunger. Sometimes, I think, 'maybe I have to pee,' so I go to the bathroom, but can't pee, so I don't think it is that. I never knew that it could mean that I was stressed out until my mom and OT taught me about stress and stomach feelings."

Phillip, a 12-year-old boy with ASD, felt vague sensations but was not able to accurately pinpoint what they meant. Many mornings, Phillip reported that he was feeling sad or depressed. His parents took him for frequent medication checks and psychological appointments, because they were concerned about the feelings he was reporting. Additionally, Phillip started working with an OT to develop self-regulation and interoceptive awareness. Through OT, Phillip and the family began tracking Phillip's reported emotions. They came to realize that he was reporting the feelings of sadness and depression mostly in the morning and that after eating breakfast, he no longer reported these feelings. Being home-schooled, Phillip habitually ate a late breakfast, a few hours after waking, because he "never was hungry."

As an experiment, Phillip started eating breakfast within 30 minutes of waking, and his reported feelings of depression and sadness reduced drastically. The family and Phillip came to realize that Phillip was misreading his interoceptive signals. He was having vague sensations that made him feel "low" or "blue," but instead of the sensations indicating sadness, they were feelings of hunger. In Phillip's case, misreading his signals had a huge impact. (Please note: Even in cases similar to Phillip's, where reduced IA causes misinterpretation of emotion/body state, feelings of depression and sadness are very real and common among individuals with ASD. If a person is reporting these feelings, always consult with a mental health professional.)

Interoceptive difficulties can have a far-reaching impact. The following sections describe this impact within specific areas.

Table 2.3
Interoceptive Discrimination Difficulty and Body States

What You Might Observe	Relation to Poor IA
When traveling, the child is asked if he needs to stop and use the bathroom. He often replies "I don't know" or "maybe."	The child truly might not know if he needs to use the bathroom. He might have a general feeling of needing the bathroom but cannot determine if he can wait or if it is an immediate need.
A child frequently complains of hunger, but when given food she only eats a bite.	The child may have mistaken the feeling of hunger for another body state like needing the toilet.
The child complains of feeling sick but cannot provide any specific symptoms.	The child may have a vague feeling of illness but cannot pinpoint the feeling to specific areas or complaints.

Interoceptive Discrimination Difficulty and Emotions

What You Might Observe	Relation to Poor IA
The child insists that she is OK even though she clearly is angry.	The child might not be able to distinguish the subtle differences in her internal body symptoms. For example, she realizes that her heart beats fast when she is very happy *and* when she is very angry. These body signals feel the same, making it difficult to distinguish between the two emotions.
The child can identify when he is angry but cannot identify the degree or intensity of the anger.	The child has a general sense of the way his body feels when he is angry; however, he does not notice the slight difference in body signals when feeling a little angry vs. really, really angry.

Self-Regulation

The inseparable connection between interoception and self-regulation was discussed in Chapter 1. From the time we are born, **interoceptive signals alert us that our balance is off and motivate us to take action, to do something that will restore the balance.** (For example, feel an itch – scratch it; feel full – stop eating; feel anxious – seek comfort). Interoception underlies our urge for action (Jackson et al., 2011). When we feel that our internal balance is off, we are motivated to act, to seek immediate relief from the discomfort caused by the imbalance. In cases of poor IA, the information underlying this urge for action is unclear or limited. Poor IA results in a dampened or non-existent urge to use a measure of self-regulation in a timely and efficient manner.

The interoceptive system drives the development of self-regulation from infancy. But without clear awareness of the interoceptive signals, effective self-regulation does not naturally develop and improve as we grow. According to Fiene and Brownlow (2015), individuals with ASD can be significantly under-aware of interoceptive signals, creating a situation where they do not clearly feel internal body sensations. This decreased IA can drastically limit the reliable information required to form effective self-regulation skills. This difficulty can extend into all forms of self-regulation and can affect many aspects of life. Let's take a closer look at two specific types of self-regulation affected when a person with ASD has reduced IA: body state regulation and emotional regulation.

Body States

As mentioned in Chapter 1, interoception and body state regulation are indivisible. That is, we rely on awareness of our interoceptive signals, or IA, to be able to detect and manage our body states. Without good IA, we would not be able regulate our most basic body functions. For example, if we do not clearly feel the sensation of a full bladder, it would be very difficult to get to a bathroom in a timely manner. Similarly, if we do not feel the sensation of a sore throat, it would be very difficult to get proper medical care, or if we misread the feeling in our abdomen to be hunger, overeating would be highly possible.

Emotion States

Challenges in the emotional domain have been considered a feature of autism since the first cases of autism reported by Leo Kanner (1943). Clinical reports point to problematic emotional responses, such as meltdowns, anxiety and/or anger outbursts, as being common among individuals with ASD (Myles & Aspy, 2016). Within the autism field, the large majority of emotion-focused studies have concentrated on the ability to recognize the emotions *in others* (Uljarevic & Hamilton, 2013). However, only a few studies have examined the ability to recognize emotions in self (e.g., Laurent & Rubin, 2004; Mazefsky et al., 2013; Myles, 2003). This leaves a large gap in our understanding of the root causes of these emotion difficulties and, in turn, impacts the development of effective intervention methods and strategies. It is proposed that one of the most common, yet overlooked, root causes of the emotion difficulties in people with ASD is poor IA. The following sections describe the connection between interoception, emotion difficulties and autism in detail.

Emotional Awareness

A vital aspect of the emotional domain involves identifying personal emotions with high levels of clarity. As we learned in Chapter 1, "feeling" emotions is important for many reasons. For example, people with good emotional awareness have better control over their emotions, demonstrate fewer instances of aggressive behaviors and have lower rates of depression.

This fine-tuned emotional awareness is an area of difficulty for many individuals with ASD (Erbas et al., 2013; Rieffe, Oosterveld, & Meerum Terwogt, 2006). That is, many demonstrate poor emotional awareness, finding it difficult to make subtle distinctions between emotions. Poor emotional awareness, clinically called *alexithymia*, involves difficulty identifying and describing emotions. Studies have found high rates of alexithymia among people with ASD, ranging as high as 65% (Berthoz & Hill, 2005; Bird & Cook, 2013; Gu, Liu, et al., 2013; Hill, Berthoz, & Frith, 2004; Samson, Huber, & Gross, 2012). Please note: This does not mean that individuals with ASD do not have emotions. That is certainly not true! Emotions are present. However, at times, they are difficult to identify with precise details.

Not surprisingly, the level of activity in the insula, which is the interoception center of the brain, is significantly correlated with scores on measures of emotional awareness. For example, studies have found that those with reduced activity in the insula scored higher on a measure of alexithymia. **In other words, low insula activity and poor emotion awareness were found in the same research participants.** Given that extensive research has shown that individuals with ASD have low insula activity, this provides a brain-level explanation of the poor emotional awareness experienced by these same individuals (Bird, Silani, Brindley,

White, Frith, & Singer, 2010; Critchley 2005; Gu, Hof, et al. 2013; Herbert et al., 2011; Silani et al., 2008).

Theories about alexithymia suggest a failure to couple or link interoceptive signals to a conscious emotional state. In other words, there is a failed connection between internal body signals and specific emotions, resulting in poor ability to identify specific emotions. Many individuals with ASD report an inability to feel or sense this connection between their interoceptive signals and emotions. Constantine, a 15-year-old with ASD, shared, *"When I was younger, I remember occasionally noticing strange sensations in my body but I never, ever considered that they were tied to emotions."*

Emotional Regulation

Over the past few years, building evidence has been pointing to impaired emotional regulation as a pervasive, universal part of ASD (Laurent & Rubin, 2004; Mazefsky et al., 2013, 2014; Samson et al., 2012; Samson, Hardan, Podell, Phillips, & Gross, 2015; Samson, Phillips, Parker, Shah, Gross, & Hardan, 2014). In other words, many, if not all, individuals with ASD have some level of difficulty regulating their emotions. Taking into account that clear, precise interoceptive information about emotions is required in order to control them (Füstos et al., 2012; Herbert et al., 2011; Lambie & Marcel, 2002; Mazefsky et al., 2013), and given that many people with ASD lack this precise interoceptive information, they are clearly missing a critical foundation for emotion regulation. Without a properly functioning interoceptive system, information about emotions may be murky or even absent. How would you know when to stop for gas if your gas gauge was broken?

- Imagine trying to control your anger if you don't realize you are angry until after you punch something (You realize you need gas only after you run out of gas in the middle of the highway … too late).

- Imagine trying to control your anxiety if you don't realize you are anxious until you are at the highest point — the full-shut-down-I-can't-take-another-second-of-this mode. (Your gauge suddenly reports that you have one mile left in the tank and you are at least fifteen miles from the nearest gas station.)

- Imagine trying to control your emotions if you have a terrible feeling all day long and report that you are really, really sad but are not sure why. After a few hours of feeling really sad and low, someone convinces you to eat something and five minutes later you magically feel better. All along you were hungry but misinterpreted the interoceptive feelings as sadness. (You are fairly sure that one of your car gauges is low, but you are not sure if it is your gas gauge, your oil gauge or your windshield wiper fluid gauge.)

In all of these instances, poor IA made it nearly impossible to use an effective strategy to control the emotion. **We need to know what emotion we are feeling in order to control it.** We could be taught hundreds and hundreds of coping strategies, but it is not until we have a clear indicator of *when* to use a strategy and *which* strategy is the best match for the emotion at hand that we will be effective emotion regulators across different situations and settings.

Without interoception providing clear feedback, it becomes difficult for individuals with ASD to develop effective ways of managing situations (Jahromi, Meek, & Ober-Reynolds, 2012; Rieffe, Oosterveld, Terwogt, Mootz, van Leeuwen, & Stockmann, 2011; Samson et al., 2012, 2014). Thus, impaired emotional regulation underlies manyof the "behaviors" commonly seen in children and adults with ASD, such as anxiety, overwhelm, meltdowns, aggression, irritability and rigidity (Mazefsky & White, 2014).

When trying to understand or interpret a challenging behavior, it is crucial to identify the underlying cause (Aspy & Grossman, 2011). Often, we look at external factors such as the environment (e.g., loud environments) or broad factors such as avoidance or escape behaviors (e.g., child typically has explosive outburst at math time in an attempt to "avoid" tasks). In these cases, we solely focus on how to modify the behavior using external means such as environmental adaptations or behavior reinforcement, missing the underlying cause, or the reason

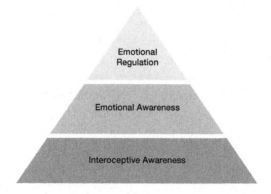

why these behaviors developed in the first place. For example, the child may have difficulty feeling the signs of building anxiety, which in turn causes her to miss an early opportunity to cope, communicate needs and/or problem-solve.

For somebody with ASD, things may quickly get out of control, making them feel completely overwhelmed. Modifying math time may help: reducing the noise in the room, teaching in a visually uncluttered area, providing reinforcement to entice participation. However, the underlying root cause of poor IA is still there, so the student will continue to have difficulty in other settings such as the cafeteria, gym class and the grocery store. No generalization will occur because the underlying cause of poor IA still remains (Aspy & Grossman).

Teaching Self-Regulation

Based on substantial research, we now know that the insula, or the interoceptive center of the brain, is significantly impacted in people with autism and that, therefore, brain-based evidence supports the interoceptive experiences reported by individuals with ASD. Taking all of this into account, we need to shift our thinking and approach self-regulation in a different manner. We need to use methods that get at the root of the cause – the underlying skill difficulty.

Without good IA, good self-regulation cannot exist. Therefore, IA needs to be a main focus when addressing self-regulation needs. The following are a few points to consider.

Decision Making and Intuition

As discussed in Chapter 1, interoception helps us learn about the world by linking experiences to how they make us feel. These interoceptive signals become a vital part of the decision-making (Damasio, 1996; Gu, Hof, et al., 2013) process. Over time, we form somatic markers (Damasio, 1994) based on the interoceptive signals/emotion that were evoked. As we go through our day, we call on these somatic markers to help us make lightning-fast predictions about the present situation, and these predictions in turn drive our decisions. Without a well-functioning interoceptive system feeding the development of somatic markers, limited information will be available for quick and intuitive decision making.

People with good IA use subtle environmental clues to make better and faster intuitive decision (Craig, 2014). Furthermore, studies have found the insula to be a main brain area involved in decision-making tasks (Gu et al., 2012; Gu, Liu, et al., 2013; Sanfey, Rilling, Aronson, Nystrom, & Cohen, 2003; Xiang et al., 2013). Therefore, reduced insula functioning, as seen in many individuals with ASD, results in a marked decrease in IA and the ability to use interoceptive signals to provide quick information about the task at hand.

Often, when poor IA causes difficulty using the intuitive, emotional process, people resort to the rational, logical thinking process to guidetheir decisions. Unfortunately, this system has major drawbacks: It is effortful and slow, and relying on it may result in reduced flexibility, difficulty adapting in uncertain environments and an inability to keep pace with rapidly changing social contexts (De Martino et al., 2008). Thus, anxiety over seemingly typical everyday situations may occur, leading to a desire for sameness and predictability.

This difficulty of making quick, intuitive decisions, especially social decisions, is a hallmark of ASD. That is, individuals with ASD often find it challenging to keep pace within social situations because the social world is fast moving, constantly changing and highly unpredictable (Klin & Volkmar, 1997; Uddin et al., 2014). Without the somatic markers to call on to quickly assess the situation and guide our intuitive actions, social situations can become overwhelming, to say the least.

Julia, a 35-year-old with ASD, shared, "For so long, I could tell you all about social skills. I knew the answer to every social skill question. I could role-play social scenarios really well. But when it came down to it, when I was in a real-life situation, it was like trying to catch up to a speeding train.

Everything moved so quickly; I was trying so hard to follow it, to think about the social rules, to think about the topic of conversation, to read the body language of others. I had to really think about all of these things. They didn't come naturally. By the time I figured out a way to join in appropriately, the others had already moved on to something else."

Table 2.4
Important Considerations for Teaching Self-Regulation to Individuals with ASD

1. **Do not skip the underlying cause.** We cannot expect a person to be able to identify personal emotions, levels, degrees or any similar concept before developing IA. A person needs to be able to feel the emotion in order to truly identify the emotion. Otherwise he is just guessing. Use the IA Builders in Chapter 4 as a starting point.
2. **Help the individual connect specific interoceptive signals to felt emotions once IA begins to emerge.** This link may not happen automatically. It needs to be taught and practiced. For ideas, refer to the IA connector tips provided in several of the IA Builders in Chapter 4.
3. **Remember the importance of feeling the subtle difference between similar emotions.** A person needs to be able to recognize the exact emotion with fine detail in order to employ a strategy that matches the emotion. Although some emotions/body states may feel similar, the subtle differences are key. An effective solution for hunger is far different from a solution for sleepiness, sadness or boredom. Start with a few body states/emotions and focus on feeling these first. As the first group is mastered, slowly increase the number.
4. **Encourage the use of specific body state and emotion terms when asking a person to identify how he feels**. For example, "I feel irritated," "I feel slightly frustrated," or "I'm really excited." This will be most functional in life. Avoid vague or abstract terminology.
5. **Accept that sometimes self-regulation strategies differ between neurotypicals and people with ASD.** The way people think and the way people see the world are sometimes different, so why wouldn't effective self-regulation strategies vary as well? Keep an open mind. Use methods to lead a person to discovering what works best. Some of the most effective self-regulation strategies have yet to be discovered.
6. **Teaching self-regulation may take a long, long time.** Be patient. Practice often. It will pay off! See tips on how to incorporate repeated practice at the conclusion of each IA Builder in Chapter 4.

Flexibility of Thought

Quick decision making and the ability to think flexibly go hand in hand. Intuitive decision making enables us to react flexibly in situations that involve a high degree of uncertainty. Without a reliable prediction system and these social instincts, it is very difficult to keep pace and go with the flow.

In the case of poor IA, when this innate prediction system and social instincts fail to develop into reliable tools, our tolerance for uncertainty decreases dramatically (Kapp, 2013). Without clear IA signals to draw on, we need to "think" through every single aspect of a situation rather than "feel" our way through certain aspects. Without these instincts at work beneath the surface allowing for automatic, unconscious behavior, each situation requires a great deal more energy. Life seems very uncertain and a lot of aspects do not naturally "make sense" or become instinctual. It is easy to see why predictability, routines and sameness would be highly desirable. For individuals with ASD, inflexibility is common and may be partly an effort to compensate for the impact of this reduced IA-based intuition.

Social Awareness and the Hidden Curriculum

Social situations are complex and unpredictable. The context is constantly changing. No two social situations are the same. Our insula is a main contributor to helping us intuitively navigate social moments (Xiang, et al., 2013). Over time, through the formation of somatic markers, interoception provides the foundation for us to naturally "know" what is expected in a given situation and, as a result, stay in line with social norms or expectations, also referred to as the hidden curriculum (Myles, Trautman, & Schelvan, 2013). This knowledge of the hidden curriculum then helps us to get by socially without the need to think through each situation. The rules become "instincts" that we can automatically call on or act on without much thought. Without this base of knowledge regarding the hidden curriculum, navigating social situations can be difficult and exhausting. Often times, individuals with ASD have great difficulty naturally learning the hidden curriculum within a wide variety of settings and contexts (Myles, et al., 2013; Vermeulen, 2012).

Perspective Taking and Empathy

As discussed in Chapter 1, interoception plays an important role in certain social cognitive skills such as perspective taking and empathy. Reduced perspective taking and empathy are considered hallmarks of ASD and are part of the core symptomatology of the diagnosis (Baron-Cohen & Wheelwright, 2004). Research has found that poor interoceptive awareness and related atypical insula function underlie these difficulties with perspective taking and empathy (Gu, Eilam-Stock, et al., 2015).

This poor awareness of one's *own* interoceptive signals, and thus emotions, directly affects the ability to predict how *others* will feel in a certain situation. Bird et al. (2010) found that individuals with high-functioning ASD (HF-ASD) with poor ability to recognize their own emotions showed significant perspective taking and empathy deficits. Furthermore, Cook, Brewer, Shah, and Bird (2013) noted that individuals with ASD who had difficulty differentiating their own emotions also had difficulty differentiating the emotions of others. Thus, the ability to recognize emotions in others is affected by how well we are acquainted with our own emotions.

In order to truly recognize and understand what someone else is feeling, we need to be aware of how it feels in ourselves first. **Therefore, interoception underlies our ability not only to answer the question, "How do I feel?" but also the question, "How do you feel?"**

Rick, a 17-year-old with high-functioning ASD, shares: "When I was younger and would see someone feeling sad, I would know that they were sad, but I had no idea just how badly they felt. I still cared about the person and did not want them to feel sad. But it wasn't until I became more aware of my interoception system and started to really feel emotions that I knew how badly sad could feel. It is much easier for me to understand how someone else is feeling now. It is much easier to connect in those moments."

Rick's comments demonstrate that if we cannot process our emotions easily, we also struggle to process emotions demonstrated by others.

Social Touch

Chapter 1 introduced a special type of touch receptor called the C Tactile fibers, or CT Fibers for short. These CT Fibers are activated by slow, gentle touch on certain areas of the body, those areas that are covered in fine hair (e.g the arm, but not the palm of the hand) (McGlone et al., 2014; Olausson et al., 2010). The interoceptive sense uses the information gathered by these CT fibers and translates the light touch into reassuring, pleasant feelings that are the foundation of social bonds.

Although we have a great deal to learn about CT fibers and the role they play in this pleasant, social touch, it has been proposed that reduced function of the social touch system can lead to light touch being aversive or distressing for individuals with ASD (Cascio et al., 2008; McGlone et al., 2014). This does not mean that all individuals with ASD find social touch to be unpleasant. That certainly is not true. However, given that the information gathered by the CT fibers land in the insula, and that the insula is commonly affected in individuals with ASD, leads researchers to question whether the dysfunctional "pleasant touch" system and the hypersensitivity to touch are linked. Only more research will reveal if an underlying disconnect of the CT fibers is a major contributor to the symptoms that individuals with ASD experience.

Awareness of Self

As presented in Chapter 1, interoception provides us with a basic sense of self (Craig, 2009; Damasio, 2010) and ownership of our own body (Herbert & Pollatos, 2012; Tsakiris et al., 2007). In other words, interoception gives us the sense that "this is me; this is my body; this is how I feel."

Many individuals with ASD describe feeling a level of disconnect from their physical bodies. They report not feeling and relating to their bodies well.

Lexie, a 25-year-old woman with ASD, shared, "Before I developed better IA, my body felt like it was not an important part of me. I did not like looking into mirrors. When I looked in the mirror, I knew intellectually that the image I saw was of me, but I didn't relate emotionally to what I saw. My reflection looked vaguely wrong, like I thought I looked different from how I really did."

The sense of self enables us to reflect upon ourselves, allowing for introspection and thus assessment of our behavior in relation to the world and others around is. So not only is interoception and self-awareness important to our ability to control the body that is ours (i.e., self-regulation) (Paulus & Stein, 2010), it forms a social foundation for how we behave and how we interact with our surroundings and interact with our surroundings (Seth, 2013). Many times individuals with autism have difficulty thinking about and making sense of themselves.

James, a 16-year-old with ASD, reported, "It has taken me years to figure out how I come across to people both socially and physically. I was often not clear on what I thought and felt. Sometimes I would have to focus on my thoughts and feelings for hours in order to reach a conclusion. My poor self-awareness made it really hard to relate not only to myself but to others."

Summary

Both research findings and personal accounts show that poor IA is common in individuals with ASD and impacts many different aspects of life. It is imperative that we learn how to best assess IA so that supports and interventions can be properly designed. The next chapter provides a comprehensive look at the assessment of the IA.

CHAPTER 3

Assessment

As we have learned, interoception is vital to self-regulation or our ability to control our various body states and emotions. Interoception is also a key foundation for many important skill areas, including decision making, self-awareness, social understanding and perspective taking. Therefore, any time a person with ASD is noted to have difficulty with any of these areas, it is important to consider poor IA as a possible underlying or root cause.

At this time, no standardized tools are available for assessing IA in its entirety (Fiene & Brownlow, 2015). However, multiple tools address specific aspects of IA. For a review of many of these tools, please refer to Mehling, Gopisetty, Daubenmier, Price, Hecht, and Stewart (2009). The following are three examples of tools that can be used to examine specific aspects of IA.

The Multidimensional Assessment of Interoceptive Awareness

The Multidimensional Assessment of Interoceptive Awareness (MAIA) is a 32-item self-report instrument (Mehling, Price, Daubenmier, Acree, Bartmess, & Stewart, 2012) that measures IA. It provides an overall picture of an individual's IA (e.g., "I notice when I am uncomfortable in my body") as well as a few emotion-specific items (e.g., "I notice how my body changes when I am angry"). The MAIA does not contain any specific questions regarding body states such as hunger. The MAIA is geared to an adult population. It can be a helpful tool to use with adults when needing a quick method to assess the need for IA intervention. However, to gain detailed information regarding how reduced IA directly impacts functional tasks, other methods of assessment will likely be needed. Currently, no studies have focused on the use of the MAIA with individuals with ASD.

The Body Awareness Questionnaire

The Body Awareness Questionnaire (BAQ; Shields, Mallory, & Simon, 1989) looks specifically at awareness of a few body states (e.g., illness: "I know I'm running a fever without taking my temperature" or sleep: "I notice distinct body reactions when I am fatigued"). The BAQ does not include any items that examine the interoception-emotion connection. Further, it was designed for college-age and adult populations and therefore is not accessible for use with children. Finally, use with individuals with ASD is limited to one recent study by Fiene and Brownlow (2015); thus, information is limited regarding the tool's effectiveness with this population.

The Toronto Alexithymia Scale

The Toronto Alexithymia Scale (TAS-20; Bagby, Parker, & Taylor, 1994) is used to assess the ability to identify and describe one's own emotions. The TAS-20 examines four factors or areas. One of the factors, called Difficulty Identifying Feelings, contains questions such as "I am often confused about what emotion I am feeling" and "I have feelings that I can't quite identify." Because it was designed to assess alexithymia, the TAS-20 does not include any items that address the interoception-body state connection. As with the BAQ, the TAS-20 was originally designed for use with adults; however, a children's version has been created by Rieffe et al. (2006).

Alternative Methods of Assessment

When assessing an adult with ASD, the MAIA, BAQ and TAS-20 may be used together to gain information about the person's IA; however, since these tools were not designed specifically for assessing IA as a whole, they may not provide a detailed view of IA. As a result, the assessor will need to use other methods, such as a guided interview, to gain all information needed.

When assessing a child with ASD, the children's version of the TAS-20 may be used (note: limited research is available regarding the use of this tool with children with ASD). The TAS-20 may provide some information regarding the child's IA as it relates to identifying his own emotions. However, since it was not designed to look specifically at IA as a whole, it will not provide information regarding body states. The assessor will need to use other methods to fill in the gaps.

Given the lack of standardized tools available for comprehensively assessing all aspects of IA, the following assessment tools were created: The Interoceptive Awareness Interview, The Assessment of Self-Regulation, and The Caregiver Questionnaire for Interoceptive Awareness.

The following pages introduce these three separate assessment tools. The assessor can choose to use one or a combination of these provided tools.

Dear Reader,

Discouraged by the lack of assessment tools available to comprehensively evaluate IA, I have spent a considerable amount of time over the past twelve years developing the following assessment tools. I have found them to be extremely helpful. Please know that these tools are a work in progress, and they are not perfected. They are updated frequently, as I am continually learning from my clients as well as from the emerging research pertaining to IA. As our knowledge regarding IA grows, it is very exciting to think about how these tools will develop and expand over time. I hope you will find them helpful.

Kelly Mahler

The Interoceptive Awareness Interview

Description: This collection of questions is designed for use in an informal, question-and-answer format. The interviewer verbally asks each question and records the respondent's answers. If the individual does better visually than auditorily, a paper copy of each question may be presented one at a time. The questions included in the IA Interview cover both awareness of body signals as they pertain to body states and awareness of body signals as they pertain to emotions.

To administer: Before starting the interview, say to the individual, "I'm going to ask you a few questions. Please answer them to the best of your ability." Then begin by asking the first Main Question and carefully listening to the answer. Record the answer in the space provided. If the person does not provide enough information via the Main Question, use the Follow-up Questions and Prompts to gain further information. If the respondent is struggling to understand or answer a question, use your best judgment to create additional questions or prompts that allow for the most information to be shared. Just be sure to remain vague and not provide any clues that reveal the answer or part of the answer in any way (e.g., OK: "How do your muscles feel when you are angry?" or "Do your muscles feel different when you are angry?" Not OK: "Do your muscles feel tight or loose when angry?").

Important Points:

- The questions are designed to guide the assessment process. No question is mandatory. Choose the questions that will provide the most information relevant to a given situation. For example, if an individual is found to have good IA as it pertains to body state regulation, then focus more on the questions related to emotions. Furthermore, when in the midst of an interview, if needed, ask a question in a different way to gain more information. The goal is to gain as much insight as possible and to end with a good picture of the individual's level of IA.

- This tool is designed for individuals who can comprehend and answer basic questions.

- For very young children or for a student of any age with a short attention span, reduce the number of questions or break the interview into chunks, providing breaks in between.

Appendix A contains the complete interview.

The Assessment of Self-Regulation

Description: This instrument was designed for use with individuals with ASD who have self-regulation difficulties. It examines an individual's understanding and thought processes surrounding aspects of self-regulation. The assessment contains a series of basic pictures that represent a variety of body states and emotions. The individual is shown a picture and asked a sequence of questions related to the picture. The questions target the following subskills of self-regulation:

- **Identifying the Body State or Emotion in Others:** What is this person feeling?

- **Identifying Causes of Body State or Emotion in Others:** What is making him/her feel that way?

- **Identifying Causes of Own Body State or Emotion:** What makes you feel this way? List at least three examples.

- **Interoceptive Awareness:** When you experience this body state/ emotion, how does your body feel? List at least three examples.

- **Strategy Identification & Problem Solving:** If you were in this situation, what would you do to feel better? List at least three examples.

The Assessment of Self-Regulation was designed to gain insight into an individual's understanding of his own body states/emotions, not the body state/emotions of others. However, when each picture is presented, the first two questions involve identifying the body state/ emotion of the person in the picture as well as the cause of the body state/emotion depicted. It is a good idea to track the accuracy with which these questions are answered because the ability to read facial expression, body language, and context and then to determine cause is important. However, it is not the main point of the assessment. There-fore, if the individual is struggling to identify the body state/emotion depicted or the cause of the body state/emotion, give her the correct answer and proceed with the remaining questions (e.g., "This boy is feeling really, really nervous because he is about to speak in public.").

To administer: Before starting the assessment, say to the individual, "I'm going to show you a few pictures and ask you questions about them. Please answer them to the best of your ability." Then begin by showing the first picture, asking the first question and carefully listening to the answer. No prompts or clues should be given. Record the answer in the space provided. If the individual does not accurately identify the body state or emotion in the picture, note this and proceed. After asking the second question, if the individual has difficulty determining the cause (trigger) of the emotion, note this on the score sheet. Before proceeding, provide the correct answer to Questions 1 and 2. Once the correct body state/emotion is determined, as well as the cause/trigger (by either the assessor or the respondent), proceed with the remaining questions and record the answers in the space provided. Do not provide answers for any of the remaining questions. Once all pictures are completed, tally the score using the master score sheet.

Important Points:

- This tool was designed for individuals with near-average receptive and expressive language abilities (e.g., can comprehend and answer basic questions).

- For very young children or older students with short attention spans, reduce the number of pictures shown or break the assessment into chunks, providing breaks in between.

- If an individual does better visually than auditorily, a paper copy of each of the questions may be presented one at a time.

Appendix B contains The Assessment of Self-Regulation as well as a master score sheet.

The Caregiver Questionnaire for Interoceptive Awareness

Description: This is a tool designed for completion by a caregiver or someone in close relation to the individual with ASD. Whenever possible, ask multiple individuals to complete the questionnaire in order to acquire information across a variety of people and environments (e.g., school and home). The questions included in the questionnaire cover both awareness of body signals as they pertain to body states and awareness of body signals as they pertain to emotions.

To administer: Provide the caregiver with a copy of the questionnaire and request answers be written in the spaces provided.

Important Points:

- The questions are designed to guide the assessment process. No question is mandatory. Choose the questions that will provide the most information relevant to each situation. Circle the questions that the caregiver is to complete. For example, if an individual is found to have good IA as it pertains to body state regulation, then circle only the questions related to emotions.

Appendix C contains the complete questionnaire.

Blank protocols for The Interoceptive Awareness Interview,
The Assessment of Self-Regulation and The Caregiver
Questionnaire for Interoceptive Awareness
are available from www.aapcpublishing.net.
Look for *The Comprehensive Assessment for
Interoceptive Awareness*.

Summary

IA provides the foundation for many crucial skills. Therefore, when supporting important skill areas such as self-regulation and social skills, it is important to assess an individual's IA. Whether using a standardized tool such as the TAS-20, or the assessment tools introduced in this chapter and presented more fully in Appendices A-C, the information gained can be used to develop a plan of action for addressing reduced IA. The following chapter provides multiple strategies for maximizing IA.

CHAPTER 4

Building Interoceptive Awareness

When I first met this sweet little seven-year-old boy named Jack, he was having a really difficult time navigating life. The referral I received read, "Full OT evaluation to address significant behavior issues." Jack's mother reported that Jack had multiple meltdowns every day. If even the slightest thing did not go Jack's way, it would cause a major emotional reaction.

Jack had been diagnosed with ASD at age five and had been through a variety of therapies with no real improvements in his behavior. Due to his difficulties and lack of progress at the public school, Jack's mom had decided to take matters into her own hands and provide his schooling within the home environment.

During my initial evaluation, I asked Jack a few questions from The Interoceptive Awareness Interview. It turned out that Jack was not able to answer even simple questions such as, "Do you ever feel stressed?" or "Do you ever feel angry?" (he was able to easily answer questions pertaining to other topics, so I knew that his difficulty was not likely language-based). When I asked Jack, "How do you feel right now?," after a long pause, he looked down at his hands and mumbled, "I don't know." In an effort to make the question less abstract, I wrote down three basic emotions (angry, happy, sad) and drew a corresponding face under each. I showed this to Jack and asked him again how he was feeling. Again his answer was, "I don't know." At that point, Jack was starting to look irritated, so I knew I had to move past these questions very quickly. I tried one more time. I wrote on two different note cards: "OK" and "Not OK" with a smiley face and frowning face, respectively, beneath each. Then I asked Jack one more time, "How do you feel right now? Do you feel OK [which I overemphasized with a really happy voice, happy face] or do you feel not OK [which I similarly overemphasized with my voice and face]?" Even with this most basic question, Jack still could not identify how he was feeling. This made me suspect that Jack had very poor IA – that he was disconnected from his body signals and emotions.

After this, we moved on to other areas of the evaluation, and during some of the fun tasks, I occasionally asked Jack questions to assess his IA (see IA on the Fly, pages 75-76) such as, "How does your heart feel after doing the jumping jacks?" Jack was not able report any changes in his body. Even when I helped him put his hand over his heart, he replied, "I don't feel anything." It was becoming clear that Jack did indeed have poor IA.

Jack's mom completed The Caregiver Questionnaire for IA, and her answers confirmed my suspicion of her son having poor IA. In addition to the emotional regulation concerns (a.k.a. "behavior issues"), she reported that Jack was unable to independently manage/interpret his body states (e.g., he never reported feeling hungry and she had to remind him to eat; toilet training was difficult, and although Jack was now fully toilet trained, she almost always had to remind him to use the bathroom). Putting all of the assessment pieces together, it was evident that poor IA was at least partly responsible for Jack's "behavior issues."

Over the next few months, Jack participated in many activities aimed at improving his IA. He created a personalized Body Check (pages 73-75), which his mom asked him to complete multiple times throughout the day. During OT sessions, activities such as How Low Can You Go? (pages 82-85) and IA on the Fly (pages 75-76) were emphasized.

Over time, Jack began showing signs of improved IA. For example, he started spontaneously to report that his heart was racing or his muscles were jumpy. With the use of an advanced Body Check, Jack began linking his observed body signals to various emotions. With his increased ability to "feel" his emotions, he was able to identify a variety of strategies to use when he experienced each emotion (these strategies had been extensively practiced during OT and at home). Jack's "behavior issues" began to drastically improve. He had significantly more control over his emotions. Over time, he began to spontaneously identify how he was feeling and could manage his emotions and body states independently. He was able to control his emotions across settings and was able to persist longer in situations that historically had been stressful to him. Jack also began reporting when he was hungry and in need of a snack or meal, which was of great significance to his mom. Additionally, Jack was more *socially in tune and started to notice and respond to others' emotional reactions with greater automaticity. With his newfound success, Jack was flourishing both emotionally and socially.*

Addressing the Underlying Cause

As illustrated in Jack's case, IA is important to many key skills. If good IA is essential to our core human experience – providing us with a clear sense of self and others (Craig, 2014) – addressing IA becomes one of the most important aspects of an effective intervention plan.

We need to be aware of our interoceptive signals in order to use them to the fullest advantage. It is evident that reduced IA can significantly impact an individual and can be the root cause of many "behavior issues." **To make gains, the underlying cause(s) must be addressed**.

Can IA Be Improved?

The good news is yes! **Research clearly shows that IA can be improved.** Furthermore, plenty of brain-based evidence shows that the insula, or the interoceptive center of the brain, can be changed for the better! Thus, after assessment, if poor IA is detected, interventions aimed at increasing IA are needed.

This chapter presents practical methods for developing effective IA. The methods can be used with a person of any age, childhood through adulthood, and can be used across a variety of settings, including home, school, clinic and community.

Two Types of Interventions for Addressing Reduced IA

Adaptations for Reduced IA

These are strategies that can be used to adapt a task in order to compensate for reduced IA. An example of an Adaptation for Reduced IA of bladder sensations is the use of discrete alarms set on a phone or other device to alert the person of when to use the bathroom throughout the day. This will allow greater independence, as the individual will not be dependent on caregiver reminders to use the bathroom.

Adaptations for Reduced IA are not intended to be used in isolation. They are designed to accommodate poor IA and increase the individual's independence, health and/or well-being. Whenever possible, also use IA Builders (see below) that specifically target the underlying poor IA. Improving IA will enable the individual to "feel" life, rather than memorizing rules, visual supports or social narratives to get by.

Examples of Adaptations for Reduced IA are provided in Appendix D. The possibilities are endless and depend on the individual situation. Therefore, create adaptations that include specific details that pertain to the situation at hand. When designing your own adaptations, be sure to incorporate the following considerations:

1. **What is the specific behavior of concern?** (e.g., needs reminders to eat on a healthy schedule; needs reminders to consistently go to the bathroom independently; does not take breaks in a setting that almost always causes overwhelm). **Please note:** Before proceeding with these adaptations, always rule out medical concerns first.

2. **What is the goal behavior?** (e.g., eats meals and snacks without adult reminders; goes to bathroom independently on a healthy schedule; takes breaks independently in overwhelming environments).

3. **What rules or specific guidelines will foster the goal behavior?** If the individual is able to participate, it is of utmost importance to include her in this process. Ask questions to discover her thoughts surrounding the goal behavior (e.g., What would make it easier for you to …?).

4. **What are the best ways to make the support concrete and visual, while respecting privacy?** Many individuals with ASD benefit from information presented in a clear, logical, visual manner. It is no different for adaptations for IA. Even though the information might be formed into a visual representation, consider methods to keep the support inconspicuous, such as a small size or private display (e.g., posted in a personal locker, not in the middle of a classroom).

5. **What technology can complement or be incorporated into the support?** This age of smartphones and portable music players makes available numerous technology-based strategies that

are both discreet and effective. An example of technology as an adaptation for IA is the use of a timer, a common feature on a smartphone, set to remind a person to go to the bathroom at set increments. Or when a person is in an environment that proves to be consistently overwhelming, the timer can be set to remind the person to take a quiet break to reduce the chance of reaching full overwhelm.

IA Builders

IA Builders are designed to promote attention to interoceptive signals. Learning to regulate one's attention in specific ways is a key feature of improving IA (see Mehling et al., 2012, for review). Thus, IA Builders are grounded in this philosophy. Over time the use of IA Builders fosters increased IA.

IA Builders are rooted in evidence-based interventions. For example, many of them employ techniques derived from mindfulness meditation, which has been shown to enhance IA (Daubenmier, Sze, Kerr, Kemeny, & Mehling, 2013; Farb, Anderson, Mayberg, Bean, McKeon, & Segal, 2010; Grossman, Niemann, Schmidt, & Walach, 2004; Khalsa, Rudrauf, Damasio, Davidson, Lutz, & Tranel, 2008). Mindfulness meditation involves "paying attention in a particular way: on purpose, in the present moment, and non-judgmentally" (Kabat-Zinn, 1994, p. 4). As such, it incorporates attention to internal body sensations such as breath, muscle tension, and heartbeat.

A brain-based explanation exists for why mindfulness can improve IA. Brain studies reveal that the insula (the interoceptive center in the brain) is strongly activated during meditation (Farb et al., 2007; Lutz, Slagter, Dunne, & Davidson, 2008). Those who participate in regular mindfulness meditation have been found to have superior insula functioning, both structurally (thicker insula) and in terms of activity levels (Farb et al., 2007; Holzel et al., 2008, 2011; Lazar et al., 2005; Lutz et al., 2008).

Given that a major premise of mindfulness meditation is **focused attention on internal body signals**, all of the IA Builders are designed to promote this type of attention. However, care needs to be taken when selecting curricula or strategies to ensure that they match the learning style of the person with ASD. Using strategies that are not designed specifically for individuals with ASD may not have the intended effect.

Simply asking a person with ASD to call attention to internal signals is often too abstract of a concept. The IA Builders attempt to make this process as concrete as possible.

In many cases, building IA is not a quick process. The journey towards true IA can be lengthy and involve considerable amounts of repeated practice. However, as in the case of Jack at the beginning of this chapter, the benefits of building IA are far reaching and life changing.

Suggested Sequence for Building IA. Below is a proposed order to follow when addressing poor IA. It is only a general recommendation. Each individual is different, has a different learning style, and will need different approaches and supports to achieve his or her goals. Therefore, following a set curriculum is highly ineffective. What works well for one individual may not work for another. Use these steps only as a loose guide. It is crucial that the needs of each individual drive this process... Listen and watch carefully, and use creativity and critical thinking to adapt concepts in this book to match each individual's unique needs.

Step 1: Introduce the concept of interoception. Interoception is a new concept for most people. Clear explanation of our eighth sensory system is important. Education of not only the individual but family members, caretakers, friends, etc., is necessary. If needed, use the handout provided in Appendix F as a guide.

Step 2: Implement adaptations for IA. Consider any areas of concern that were identified through the assessment process. If any of these areas need to be addressed immediately, for example, if the concern is greatly impacting the health, safety or independence of an individual, implement adaptations for IA where applicable (e.g., mirror checks for injuries, alert on smartphone for bathroom breaks or meal times).

Step 3: Build IA. This step involves using a collection of IA Builders to develop IA and may require extensive time and practice. **When learning a new skill, power often comes from repeated practice.** Developing IA is no different. When using the IA Builders, repeated, guided practice is important. In almost every situation, it is not enough to teach the strategy or skill once and expect it to make a difference. Sometimes, it is not even enough to use or practice the strategy or skill ten times or even one hundred times to make a difference. In order to reach a level of mastery, practice has to occur until critical mass is achieved. Critical mass occurs when one has had enough practice and experience to generate one's own knowledge about a particular topic (personal communication, Brenda Myles, April 15, 2015). Therefore, repeated practice of the IA Builders is absolutely essential. Refer to the Repeated Practice Opportunity suggestions provided for each IA Builder.

Step 4: Give IA meaning. Once an individual develops a basic awareness of interoceptive signals (e.g., feeling her heart race, muscle tighten or stomach "growl"), begin to give these sensations meaning. Using a structured format, as in the IA Connector Form (Appendix E), demonstrate how each sensation or collection of sensations equals an emotion or body state. For example, Heavy Muscles + Foggy Brain + Slow Heart + Droopy Eyelids = Tired. This connection between body signals and body state/emotion may be obvious for some individuals, but for others, it will need to be clearly explained and practiced many times. At first, focus on identifying a few body states/emotions, but as the individual grows in this process, expand upon the body states/emotions until an extensive repertoire is achieved.

> **Tip:** Use functional, real-life terms when connecting IA to emotions and body states (e.g., "I feel...irritated, tired, angry, bored or hungry").

Step 5: Use IA to maximize related skills. Once an individual develops a basic level of IA and is using interoceptive signals to identify body states and emotions, use this new foundation to maximize skills such as self-regulation and social interaction. For example, IA is an often overlooked, yet absolutely vital aspect of self-regulation. We have to know how we are feeling in order to control it. Therefore, once an individual has achieved a basic level of IA, successful self-regulation becomes a realistic goal. This is the point when different coping strategies can be linked to each emotion or body state (e.g., when I feel hungry, I can do this ...; when I feel angry, I can do this ...). Support the individual in discovering strategies that may be personally unique to the individual (use activities such as How Low Can You Go? [pages 82-85] to foster this process). Additionally, provide and trial a wide variety of coping strategies. This will allow an individual to find out which strategies are most effective and preferable.

The following pages provide Adaptations for Reduced IA, followed by IA Builders. Designed to be a guide, please adapt them to meet individual needs and learning styles.

Adaptations for Reduced IA

The Adaptations for Reduced IA are based upon strategies that are already included in most interventions for individuals with ASD. Both visual supports and social narratives are widely talked and written about in autism literature. Thus, this section is notably shorter than the subsequent section that provides IA Builders. For more information regarding visual supports or social narratives, please refer to http://www.txautism. net/target-texas-autism-resource-guide-for-effective-teaching.

Visual Supports

Visual supports are tools that provide predictability and decrease anxiety about the unknown. For example, a visual schedule takes an abstract concept (e.g., time) and presents it in a more concrete form using words and/or pictures. Visual supports not only help by making expectations clear, they can serve as visual reminders to complete a task. For more information please refer to http://www.txautism.net/target-texas-autism-resource-guide-for-effective-teaching. Visual supports should be highly individualized and a match for each individual student and situation. Use the samples in Appendix D only as a guide.

Social Narratives

A social narrative is a short story that teaches or clearly describes a situation and the related expectations. These short stories take an often abstract concept and break it down into clear and manageable parts. The expectations are explained and frequently a rationale is included (e.g., why a given behavior is important). For more information, please refer to   http://www.txautism.net/target-texas-autism-resource-guide-for-effective-teaching. Social narratives should be highly individualized and a match for each individual student and situation.

IA Builders

IA Builder 1: Body Check

Prerequisite: None. The Body Check is a great introductory activity. It is recommended that all individuals create and use a Body Check.

Materials Needed:
- Supplemental Materials from Appendix E
- Large piece of butcher paper (size of student's body) *or* copy of the body outline from Appendix E
- Pencils
- Markers
- Construction paper in various colors
- Laminator (recommended but optional)
- Velcro (recommended but optional)

Directions:

To make the visual support that will guide the Body Check

1. Before meeting with the individual, decide which version of the body check to make.

   Large version: Created from outlining the individual's body; it is a very large product and less portable; however, it provides a concrete connection for the individual: This is *my* body, I am thinking about *my* body.

   Small version: Created by using the generic body outline from Appendix E; it is small and portable but does not provide a concrete representation of *"my* body," which certain individuals need to make the connection.

2. If you are making the large version, have the individual lie down and trace his body on a large sheet of butcher paper. If you are making the small version, have a blank version of the body outline from Appendix E ready to use.

3. Taking into account the individual's level of IA and cognition, determine the number of body symptoms to initially incorporate into the Body Check. To avoid overwhelming the individual, start with a few and gradually increase the number. A list of suggested body symptoms are provided in Appendix E.

4. In collaboration with the individual, use construction paper to make small shapes that estimate the body parts that correlate with the body symptoms selected from Step 3. For ideas on what shapes

to use, see pictures in Appendix E; however, use the individual's ideas for best results. Make multiple copies of each body part.

5. Label each of the body parts with descriptor words that are meaningful to the individual. For examples, refer to Appendix E. Also include a blank version of each body part so that the individual will have the option of identifying a new descriptor when completing future Body Checks.

6. Optional, but suggested: Laminate each of the body parts as well as the body outline. Add one side of Velcro to the back of the body parts, and the opposite side of the Velcro to points on the Body Outline that approximate the location of each corresponding part (see Appendix E for an example).

To complete a Body Check:

1. Start by selecting one body part with the individual (e.g., hands). Encourage the individual to focus on that body area and think about how the particular area feels. The individual should then select that body part with the corresponding descriptor (e.g., sweaty palms) and place it in the body outline at the appropriate spot (see Appendix E for an example). The individual may also select the blank version of the particular body part, if he feels something different than expressed by the descriptors provided. Be sure to offer plenty of prompts that encourage the individual to focus his awareness on the specific body part and to focus on how it feels before selecting the choice.

2. Continue the Body Check by moving through each remaining body parts following the instructions in Step 1.

3. **Repeated Practice Opportunity:** The Body Check is designed to be used multiple times throughout the day. When starting, it is best to use it only during periods of calm or in positive situations. Slowly advance to doing Body Checks during mild body states or emotions such as sleepy times, hungry times, antsy times, minimally frustrated times. Once it becomes a habit, and if the individual agrees, try it during more intense body states and/or emotions.

4. **Remember:** If the Body Check is too difficult or overwhelming, reduce the number of body parts the individual has to check. Even one body part is OK to start with! As the individual improves, gradually add more body parts.

5. **IA Connector:** As the individual grows proficient in completing a Body Check during multiple situations and environments, begin

to connect the sensations to body states and emotions. Clearly teach and show the individual the relationship between internal body signals and body states/emotions (use IA Connector form in Appendix E). As the individual identifies sensations during a Body Check, guide her in adding the sensations together and pinpointing the exact body state or emotion. In the beginning, adding a list of body states and emotions on the back of the Body Check chart may be helpful. Start with a short list of basic terms. As the individual progresses, the list of terms can grow as well. The more body states and emotions the individual can differentiate between the better.

IA Builder 2: IA on the Fly

Prerequisite: None

Materials Required:
• Supplemental Materials from Appendix E

Directions:
1. During a specific moment, take a quick pause and ask the individual to describe how her overall body *or* specific body parts feel in that moment. Use the worksheet from Appendix E for suggested situations and questions to use in order to help the individual attend to the internal signals.
2. If an individual might benefit from a visual support to help guide this activity, use the body outline created in IA Builder 1: Body Check.
3. **Repeated Practice Opportunity:** Use this strategy frequently. It encourages the individual to attend to the internal signals. In order to make this a natural process for her, the individual may need to do this activity with support many, many times. Try this strategy across situations and environments. It does not require a lot of time or materials, and the payoff is huge.
4. **IA Connector:** As the individual gets proficient at describing a variety of sensations during multiple situations and environments, begin to connect the sensations to body states and emotions. Clearly teach and show the individual the relationship between internal body signals and body states/emotions (use form in Appendix E). As the individual identifies sensations during IA on the Fly, guide him in adding the sensations together and

pinpointing the exact body state or emotion. Providing a list of body states and emotions may be helpful in the beginning. Start with a short list of basic terms. As the individual progresses, the list of terms can grow as well. The more body state and emotions the individual can differentiate between the better.

IA Builder 3: Body Scan

Prerequisite: Body Check

Materials Required:
- Supplemental Materials from Appendix E
- Wand, stick, light saber

Directions:
1. When an individual is in a calm and focused state, begin by saying, "We are going to learn how to do a Body Scan today. It is a helpful way to notice different feelings from the inside of your body. I'm going to use this cool wand/stick/light saber to help us along."
2. Have the individual sit or lie down in a comfortable position.
3. Say to the individual, "I'm going to use my cool wand/stick/light saber to scan different parts of your body." (Tip: If the individual does not understand the concept of scan, compare it to a photocopier light that scans the document before printing or refer to the scans performed by the character Baymax from the Disney movie *Big Hero 6*.) "The wand will never touch you. When I stop the wand over a certain area in your body, I want you to tell me what you feel in that area. If it is tricky, I'll help you."
4. Moving from head to toe, begin by holding the wand over the individual's forehead. Do NOT make contact with the individual; the wand should always hover a few inches above the area of focus. Use the suggested prompts below or create your own. Start with vague prompts and move to more specific ones if the individual struggles. If the individual is still unable to give an answer after prompts, move on to the next body part.
   General Prompts:
   - What do you feel here?
   - What body part(s) is located in this area?
   - What does your ____(body part) feel like?

Specific Prompts:
- Does your ____(body part) feel _____(descriptor examples; e.g., fast, swirly, focused, distracted, heavy, fuzzy, blank, stuck)?

5. Continue moving the wand from top to bottom of the individual's body, pausing at various areas and repeating Step 4. See Appendix E for list of suggested stopping points.
6. **Important Note:** Use your judgment in terms of the number of areas focused on during the first Body Scan. If the individual is doing well, provide challenge by pausing at many of the suggested points. If the individual is struggling, pause at only a few areas.
7. **Optional:** Use the Instructor Guide (see Appendix E) to record the individual's responses and level of prompts to track improvements.
8. **Repeated Practice Opportunity:** With adult support, have the individual complete a Body Scan multiple times a day. As the individual makes gains, increase the number of focus areas. Once an individual is proficient with this process, encourage independent Body Scans by using the Independent Body Scan form (either text version or body outline version) found in Appendix E.

IA Builder 4: Let It Out!

Prerequisite: This is an advanced activity. The individual should be comfortable completing independent Body Scans and/or body checks.

Materials Needed:
- Voice recorder or paper and pen
- Supplemental Materials from Appendix E

Directions:
1. **Important Note:** Very often, individuals with ASD report difficulty recalling the details of dysregulated periods. Therefore, having them record observations when "in the moment" can be helpful. *This is a difficult strategy to use.* Some individuals find it uncomfortable or even impossible to record observations when in a heightened emotional state; however, those who can record observations can use this information to gain better control over intense body states or emotions.

2. In collaboration with the individual, place a voice recorder or pen and paper in a space that allows easy access. Also, a visual support from Appendix E (either the text version or body outline version) displayed in the same space may serve as a helpful guide to the "let it out" process (see below).

3. When the individual begins to experience a heightened body state or emotion, ask him to either voice record (typically preferred method) or write down his observations regarding the different sensations located in various areas of the body. Grammar, spelling, sentence structure, etc., are not relevant in this activity. The focus is getting thoughts, feelings and observations recorded for later use.

4. **Important Note:** Before trying this strategy, it is important that all parties acknowledge the possibility that "inappropriate" language and/or content will be part of the recorded observation. The recordings are taken when the individual is in a heightened state where thinking is not clear or focused on what is socially appropriate. The goal is to get the individual's observations, feelings and thoughts recorded for use when creating self-regulation strategies. Therefore, limiting restrictions will allow the individual to feel free to truly "let it all out."

IA Builder 5: Focus Areas

Prerequisite: None. These activities will help to foster growth on Body Check, Body Scan or IA on the Fly.

Materials Needed:
  • Varies, depending on focus area and activities selected

Directions:
1. This activity is designed to promote awareness of a single body area and the related sensations. As the individual uses the Body Check, Body Scan or IA on the Fly strategies, note the body symptoms that are the most challenging and use this information when selecting the areas that need the most practice and attention. For example, if an individual is unable to report how her heart feels, then the heart should be a focus area. If the individual is unable to report how her muscles feel, then muscles should be a focus area.

2. Select one focus area from the list below (or come up with your own):

Brain	Skin
Eyes	Breathing
Nose	Heart
Cheeks	Stomach
Mouth/Jaw	Muscles
Voice	Hands and fingers
Ears	Feet and toes

3. Create activities or experiments that promote awareness of a particular body area and related sensations. Some examples are provided in Appendix E, but many options are available. Use creativity and incorporate the individual's interests and ideas whenever possible.

4. During all activities and experiments, ALWAYS emphasize attention to internal body sensations. Encourage the individual to frequently attend to and "feel" his body and describe with specificity the body sensations noted.

IA Builder 6: The Heartbeat Games

Prerequisite: None. This is a great activity for developing awareness of one's heart.

Materials Required:
- Supplemental Materials (see Appendix E)
- Suggested Activity List (see Appendix E)
- Stopwatch or timer
- Pulse-oximeter ("pulse-ox;" may be purchased from Amazon.com for around $20)

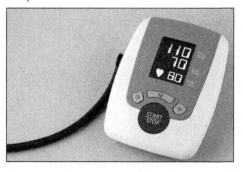

Directions:

1. Begin the activity by saying, "We are going to do a few fun experiments to examine what happens to your heart after you complete different activities. Before we start, I'm going to put this pulse-ox on your finger. It is a really cool gadget that measures how fast or slow your heart is beating. It does not hurt; it just puts a little bit of pressure on your finger."

2. Put the pulse-ox on the individual's index finger according to package directions.

3. Wait for the pulse-ox to measure the first heart rate. Once the heart rate appears on the screen, if needed, explain to the individual exactly what the number means (e.g., "This is how many times your heart beats in 1 minute").

4. Help the individual record the heart rate in the designated space on the worksheet provided in Appendix E.

5. Continue by guiding the individual through each activity listed on the worksheet and recording the measured heart rate in the designated spaces. For activity ideas, see Suggested Activity List in Appendix E.

6. **Maximizing the Connection to IA:** Once the individual is familiar with the Heartbeat Games, start to encourage the individual to increase his attention to his heart; that is, try **feeling** the heart beat. This is typically easiest after intense activity (see examples in Appendix E) when the heart is racing. Prompt the individual to "feel" his heart. Use questions such as, "What does your heart feel like right now?" or "Can you feel your heart beating?" If this is difficult, have the individual put his hand over his heart to help him "feel" it better. As the individual becomes more successful with this process, try calling attention to the sensation at different activity levels.

7. **Repeated Practice Opportunity**: Repeat the Heartbeat Games frequently, exploring a variety of activities with the individual. Do this during structured, planned opportunities as well as on-the-spot opportunities (e.g., after recess or riding bike).

IA Builder 7: Guess Your Heart Rate

Prerequisite: The individual should be familiar with and have shown repeated progress on IA Builder 6: Heartbeat Games

Materials Required:
- Supplemental Materials (see Appendix E)
- Pulse-oximeter (may be purchased from Amazon.com for around $20)

Directions:
1. Begin the activity by saying, "Now that you are an expert at the Heartbeat Games, we are going to try something even trickier and even more fun. You are going to try to guess your heart rate without the pulse-ox. After you make a guess, we will use the pulse-ox to see how close you are. Remember, this is really tricky, so if you are not close, it is OK! Let's have fun!"
2. Have the individual guess her heart rate and help her record it in the designated space on the worksheet from Appendix E. If needed, provide prompts to help her make a smart guess. Encourage the individual to "feel" her heart, to really think about it, and make a good guess.
3. Put the pulse-ox on the individual's index finger according to package directions.
4. Wait for the pulse-ox to measure the first heart rate.
5. Record the heart rate on the designated space on form.
6. Calculate the difference between the guessed heart rate and the actual heart rate and help the individual record the difference in the designated spot on the worksheet.
7. **Maximizing the Connection to IA:** Remember, the goal is to increase awareness of the heart and related sensations. During all practice opportunities, prompt the individual to "feel" her heart. Use questions such as, "What does your heart feel like right now?" or "Can you feel your heart beating?" If this is difficult, have the individual put her hand over her heart to help her "feel" it better.
8. **Repeated Practice Opportunity:** Repeat the Guess Your Heart Rate activity numerous times – during structured, planned opportunities as well as on-the-spot opportunities (e.g., after recess or riding bike). Challenge the individual to beat her record, coming as close to the actual heart rate as possible.

IA Builder 8: How Low Can You Go?

Prerequisite: The individual should be familiar with IA Builder 6: Heart-beat Games.

Materials Required:
- Supplemental Materials (see Appendix E)
- Suggested Activity List (Appendix E)
- Stopwatch or timer
- Pulse-oximeter (may be purchased from Amazon.com for around $20)

Directions:
1. Begin the activity by saying, "We're going to play a fun game called How Low Can You Go?. You will start by doing something really active for 60 seconds. As soon as you finish, I will put the pulse-ox on your finger."
2. Have the individual complete 60 seconds of an intense activity (see Appendix E for suggested activities).
3. Immediately put the pulse-ox on the individual's index finger according to package directions.
4. Wait for the pulse-ox to measure the first heart rate.
5. Record the heart rate in the designated space on the worksheet from Appendix E and quickly move to Step 6.
6. Challenge the individual by saying, "Here is the challenge: Keep the pulse-ox on your finger. You have 60 seconds to slow your heart rate. You can do whatever you need to do in order to get it as low as possible. Ready, go!" Do not provide any ideas or additional prompts (see below). Start the timer for 60 seconds. With the pulse-ox on her finger, the individual will receive clear feedback regarding the strategies attempted throughout the 60 seconds.
7. **Important Note:** Speed and vague directions are both vital aspects of this activity, especially the first time. Speed is important so that the individual's heart rate is still fast once he begins trying to lower the heart rate. This will allow for the biggest drop, providing the highest chance for a successful first attempt. Vague directions allow for observations regarding what the individual will naturally and independently do to lower his heart rate.
8. During the 60 seconds, observe the individual carefully. Remember, do not prompt the individual or give any feedback! Note each strategy attempted as well as the outcome of each (e.g., What did

the individual do to lower heart rate? What was his first instinct? Was it successful? Did the individual alter the strategy if it did not slow the heart? Did the individual demonstrate a clear ability to or knowledge of how to calm his body and heart?).

9. After the 60 seconds, record the heart rate on the form provided.

10. Very often, it is difficult for an individual with poor IA to fully lower his heart rate without help. If that is the case, proceed as follows.

11. After the initial 60-second challenge, the activity can be continued with a little more support. Say to the individual, "We are going to try this again, but this time I am going to help you a little bit. You have 60 more seconds to get your heart as slow as possible."

12. Start the time for another 60 seconds. Do not give the individual answers! Only provide prompts (e.g., "Is what you are doing working?" "What else could you try?" "I see you walking around, what else could you do with your body?"), but do not give the individual direct answers. This is important for two reasons:

- Allowing the individual to discover the best ways to lower the heart rate through trial and error helps her learn a problem-solving process that is similar to real life. For example, when we feel upset we might try to repair our feelings via a certain method (e.g., seeking help or taking a deep breath), and it might not work. We then have to have other ideas or a back-up plan to try (e.g., talking to a friend, retreating to a quiet space) ... and we might have to keep trying different methods until we feel better.

- Individuals with ASD might have different ideas for strategies, strategies that neurotypicals might not ever consider. This trial-and-error process may allow for a unique strategy to emerge. Watch carefully and ask questions to discover exactly what the individual was thinking throughout each 60-second segment. What works for a neurotypical does not necessarily work for a person with ASD. Take, for example, deep breathing. It is a widely accepted coping strategy, but for some people it is not effective.

Jo, a 14-year-old with ASD, would report feelings of panic when trying to implement deep breathing techniques. He was following the proper protocols for deep breathing, but it still caused him to have an increased heart rate. Once this strategy was abandoned and Jo was encouraged to find other calming methods, he was able to find several methods that worked for him. He simply needed to be guided to find his own strategies in a structured and supportive manner.

13. **Repeated Practice Opportunity:** Repeat this activity multiple times across situations and environments. Continue until the individual is able to consistently lower the heart rate using several different methods.

    Note: This activity is a great way to start the school day or to start out a therapy session as it gets the individual calm, centered and ready to "work." It also can be a great activity to do before bed as it provides a concrete way to slow the heart, relax the body and focus the brain.

14. **Maximizing IA:** Once the individual becomes comfortable with How Low Can You Go?, begin incorporating prompts/questions at certain points that encourage him to attend to various body sensations. The following are examples.
    * Encourage the individual to describe the way his heart feels at the start of the activity, after the intense activity and at the end of the 60-second cooldown. Compare and contrast.
    * Encourage the individual to describe the way his breathing changes throughout this activity.
    * Encourage the individual to describe the way his muscles change throughout this activity.

IA Builder 9: How Low Can You Go? – Advanced

Prerequisite: Mastery of How Low Can You Go?

Materials Required:
  * Supplemental Materials (see Appendix E)
  * Suggested Activity List
  * Stopwatch or timer
  * Pulse-oximeter (may be purchased from Amazon.com for around $20)
  * Group of students (optional)

Directions:
1. Begin the activity by saying, "Now that you are all experts at How Low Can You Go?, we're going to increase the challenge in a really fun way. First, we need one person to be 'it.' Any volunteers?" (Pause and select volunteer.)

2. Continue by saying, "The individual who is 'it' will do twenty jumping jacks. After the jumping jacks, we will measure her heart rate using the pulse-ox. Then begins the challenge. The individual who is 'it' will have 60 seconds to slow her heart rate as low as she can go. There is a catch! The rest of you will have an important job … your job is to distract her, to keep her from slowing her heart. The only rules are that you may not touch her at any time and you must remain respectful."

3. After making sure that everyone understands the directions, have the individual who is "it" complete twenty jumping jacks (or any intense activity; see Appendix E for suggestions).

4. Immediately put the pulse-ox on her index finger according to package directions.

5. Wait for the pulse-ox to measure the first heart rate.

6. Quickly record the heart rate in the designated space on the worksheet from Appendix E and move to Step 7.

7. Instruct the individual who is "it" to start working to lower her heart rate. Instruct the others to begin distracting her (ideas include making strange noises, singing an annoying song, flashing the lights, saying funny things, walking in a circle around the individual). Start the timer for 60 seconds.

8. During the 60 seconds, carefully observe the individual who is "it." Do not prompt the individual or give any feedback (see IA Builder 8: How Low Can You Go?). Note each strategy attempted as well as the outcome of each (e.g., What did the individual do to lower heart rate? What was his first instinct? Was it successful? Did the individual alter the strategy if it did not slow his heart? Did the individual demonstrate a clear ability to or knowledge of how to calm his body and heart?).

9. After the 60 seconds, record the ending heart rate on the form provided in Appendix E. Calculate the drop in heart rate and also record on the form.

10. Repeat Steps 2-7 until everyone has a turn being "it."

11. Results can be used in two ways:
    • On-the-spot winner: The individual who demonstrated the biggest drop in heart rate wins.
    • Tracking progress over time: Each time an individual completes the challenge, track her individual performance and celebrate improved scores.

12. Once each individual has had a turn and the results are revealed, discuss with the group the various strategies that were used to lower the heart and block out distractions. Reflect on the level of success of each strategy. Discuss methods to implement the most successful strategies during real-life situations. Listen carefully and gain insight into possible strategies that might not have been considered in the past.

13. **Repeated Practice Opportunity:** Do this activity multiple times using a variety of distractors and environments. Continue until each individual is able to consistently lower her heart rate using multiple methods.

14. **Very Important Note:** If an individual is overresponsive to certain sensations, ALWAYS respect these sensory sensitivities. Due to the variety of distractions used, like intense sounds, this activity may be aversive to some.

IA Builder 10: Dueling Hearts

Prerequisite: Mastery of How Low Can You Go?

Materials Required:
- Supplemental Materials (see Appendix E)
- Stopwatch or timer
- Two pulse-oximeters (may be purchased from Amazon.com for around $20)
- Group of individuals (at least two)

Directions:
1. Begin the activity by saying, "Now that you are all experts at How Low Can You Go?, we are going to increase the challenge in a really fun way. First, I need two people to be 'it.' Any volunteers?" (Pause and select volunteers.)

2. Continue by explaining to the two volunteers, "The two of you will go head-to-head for 60 seconds, trying to lower your heart rate. The individual who has the biggest drop at the end wins."

3. After making sure that everyone understands the directions, have the two individuals who are "it" complete twenty jumping jacks (or any other intense activity; see Appendix E for suggestions).

4. Immediately put a pulse-ox on each individual's index finger according to package directions.

5. Wait for the pulse-ox to measure the heart rates.

6. Quickly record the heart rates in the designated space on the worksheet from Appendix E and move to Step 7.
7. Instruct the individuals to start working to lower their heart rate. Start the timer for 60 seconds. Do not provide ideas or prompts! (See How Low Can You Go?)
8. During the 60 seconds, carefully observe the individuals who are "it." Again, do not prompt or give any feedback. Note each strategy attempted as well as the outcome of each (e.g., What did each individual do to lower heart rate? What was each individual's first instinct? Was it successful? Did each individual alter the strategy if it did not slow his heart? Did each individual demonstrate a clear ability to calm his body and heart?).
9. After the 60 seconds, record both heart rates on the form provided in Appendix E. Calculate the drop in heart rate and also record on the form.
10. Announce results: The individual who demonstrated the biggest drop in heart rate wins.
11. **Repeated Practice Opportunity:** Do this activity multiple times in a variety of settings. Add distractors to increase the challenge (see IA Builder 9: How Low Can You Go? – Advanced for ideas). Continue until the dueling individuals are able to consistently lower their heart rate using multiple methods.

IA Builder 11: Breathing Games

Prerequisite: None. This is a great activity to foster increased awareness of the breath

Materials Required:
*   Supplemental Materials (see Appendix E)
*   Suggested Activity List (see Appendix E)
*   Stopwatch
*   Amplifier (e.g., Forebrain, DIY phonics phone, DIY whisper phone; http://teacherificfun.blogspot.com/2013/02/diy-whisper-phones. html; toy microphone)

Directions:
1. Begin the activity by saying, "We're going to do a few fun experiments to see how your breathing changes during different activities."

2. Help the individual find a comfortable position (sitting or lying down) and encourage him to close his eyes and breathe normally.
3. Encourage the individual to describe the sensations noted surrounding the breathing. Use guiding questions such as, "When you breathe, what do you feel? What feelings do you notice in your chest? Nose? Mouth?" Do not provide prompts.
4. Have the individual take a few deep breaths and describe the difference in sensations with deep breathing. Do not provide prompts. If the individual is struggling, move on to Step 5, using the amplifier to increase feedback and allow for better awareness.
5. Using the amplifier, have the individual breathe normally and describe her observations. Then try deep breathing and have her describe the observations. In order to build IA, emphasize attention to the sensations in the body.
6. After completing the above introductory activities, use the worksheet from Appendix E to guide the remainder of the activity. Also refer to Appendix E for suggested activities at each intensity level.
7. **Repeated Practice Opportunity:** Do this activity, or portions of it, multiple times. Continue until the individual is able to consistently notice and describe difference in breathing.

IA Builder 12: Squeeze and Loosen

Prerequisite: None. This is a good activity to focus awareness on the muscles.

Materials Required:
• Supplemental Materials (see Appendix E)

Directions:
1. Begin the activity by saying, "Our muscles can change all of the time. Sometimes, muscles are tight, sometimes muscles are loose, sometimes muscles are tired, and sometimes muscles are sore.

Muscles can feel many different ways. Today, we are going to play a fun game that involves feeling our muscles."

2. Place the game cards from Appendix E face down in two piles on a table or the floor. Pile 1 should contain all cards with muscle or body part names. Pile 2 should contain the cards with "Squeeze" or "Loosen."

3. Have the individual select one card from each pile. The individual is to replicate the action on the card from Pile 2 with the muscles listed on the card from Pile 1 (e.g., if the individual selects "Squeeze" and "Forehead," he is to tense the muscles in his forehead tightly).

4. Both before, during and after the individual performs the action, use guiding questions to focus his attention on the sensations provoked (e.g., "How do the muscles in your forehead feel while you are squeezing them? How do the muscles in your forehead feel after you release them? Describe the difference.").

5. Continue the activity until all cards are used.

6. **Repeated Practice Opportunity:** Spontaneously, have the individual do one- or two-card combinations at various times. Work on building the speed with which the individual can perform the action as well as how well he is able to describe the sensations evoked by various card combinations.

IA Builder 13: Interoception in Others

Prerequisite: Good performance on Body Check, Body Scan and/or IA on the Fly. The individual should have a good awareness of personal interoceptive signals and emotions/body states before moving to inferring the interoceptive signals and emotion/body states of others.

Materials Required:
- Supplemental Materials (see Appendix E)
- Pictures and/or videos of people demonstrating various emotions in a variety of contexts

Directions:
1. Begin the activity by showing the individual the first picture or video clip.
2. Have the individual infer the interoceptive signals of the person in the picture/video. This can be done verbally, by completing a Body

Check or by labeling body sensations on a blank body outline (see Appendix E).

3. **IA Connector:** Once the individual correctly identifies the interoceptive signals of the person in the picture/video, have her connect the sensations to a body state(s) and/or emotion(s). Clearly depict the relationship between internal body signals and body states/emotions by using the IA Connector form in Appendix E. Once the body sensations are added together, have the individual identify the body state(s)/emotions(s) depicted in the picture. Expand the individual's ability to use a wide range of body state and emotion terms. At first, it may be helpful to provide a list of body states and emotions.

IA Builder 14: How Do I Feel?

Prerequisite: Good performance on Body Check, Body Scan and/or IA on the Fly.

Materials Required:
• Supplemental Materials (see Appendix E)

Directions:
1. Begin the activity by placing the game cards (see Appendix E) face down on the table.
2. The player to go first selects and looks at the first card, not showing it to any other players.
3. The player with the first game card verbally gives a list of body sensations typically connected with the given body state or emotion stated on the card. For example, if the emotion on the game card is "nervous," the individual may say "shaking muscles, fast heart, cold hands, tingly stomach."
4. Based on the sensations provided, the remaining players try to guess the body state/emotion listed on the game card.
5. Once somebody guesses the correct body state/emotion, the next player selects a game card and follows Step 3-4.
6. Proceed in the same manner until all game cards have been used.

Summary

The strategies in this chapter will provide a great starting point for building IA. Whenever possible, adapt the activities to match the unique needs and interests of each individual. The journey toward effective IA may take time, but the payoff is huge.

CHAPTER 5

A Need for Change

The evidence showing just how important interoception, our eighth sensory system, is to many aspects of our life is unequivocal. My hope is that the chapters in this book have challenged the current thinking surrounding many important skill areas such as self-regulation, self-awareness and social understanding. Given that over 90% of adults with autism are under- or unemployed and are unable to live independently (Barnard, J., Harvey, V., Potter, D., & Prior, A., 2001), mostly due to poor self-regulation, self-awareness and/or social understanding, we must be actively searching for those missing components that will drive successful interventions.

Could IA be a missing link? The evidence seems to suggests so. This realization can be used for the good, to further our thinking and further the interventions used to help individuals with autism. This book serves as an opener to this conversation. We have a lot more to learn. Hopefully, the information presented in this book will become widespread across the autism community and, in turn, push a new wave of ideas and research.

Progress is impossible without change, and those that cannot change their minds cannot change anything.

—George Bernard Shaw

References

American Psychiatric Association (2013). *Diagnostic and statistical manual of mental disorders* (5th ed.). Washington, DC: Author.

Aspy, R., & Grossman, B. (2011). *Designing comprehensive interventions for high-functioning individuals with autism spectrum disorders: The Ziggurat model-Release 2.0.* Shawnee Mission, KS: AAPC Publishing.

Bagby, R. M., Parker, J. D., & Taylor, G. J. (1994). The twenty-item Toronto Alexithymia Scale I. Item selection and cross-validation of the factor structure. *Journal of Psychosomatic Research, 38*(1), 23-32.

Baker, A.E.Z., Lane, A., Angley, M. T., & Young, R. L. (2008). The relationship between sensory processing patterns and behavioral responsiveness in autistic disorder: A pilot study. *Journal of Autism and Developmental Disorders, 38*, 867-875.

Baranek, G. T., David, F. J., Poe, M. D., Stone, W. L., & Watson, L. R. (2006). Sensory experiences questionnaire: Discriminating sensory features in young children with autism, developmental delays, and typical development. *Journal of Child Psychology and Psychiatry, 47*(6), 591-601.

Barnard, J., Harvey, V., Potter, D., & Prior, A. (2001). *Ignored or ineligible? The reality for adults with autism spectrum disorders.* London: National Autistic Society.

Baron-Cohen, S., & Wheelwright, S. (2004). The empathy quotient: An investigation of adults with Asperger syndrome or high functioning autism, and normal sex differences. *Journal of Autism and Developmental Disorders, 34*(2), 163-175.

Barrett, L. F., Quigley, K. S., Bliss-Moreau, E., & Aronson, K. R. (2004). Interoceptive sensitivity and self-reports of emotional experience. *Journal of Personality and Social Psychology, 87*(5), 684.

Barrett, L. F., Gross, J., Christensen, T. C., & Benvenuto, M. (2001). Knowing what you're feeling and knowing what to do about it: Mapping the relation between emotion differentiation and emotion regulation. *Cognition & Emotion, 15*(6), 713-724.

Bechara, A., & Damasio, A. R. (2005). The somatic marker hypothesis: A neural theory of economic decision. *Games and Economic Behavior, 52*(2), 336-372.

Bechara, A., Damasio, H., Tranel, D., & Damasio, A. R. (2005). The Iowa Gambling Task and the somatic marker hypothesis: Some questions and answers. *Trends in Cognitive Sciences, 9*(4), 159-162.

Bechara, A., Damasio, H., Tranel, D., & Damasio, A. R. (1997). Deciding advantageously before knowing the advantageous strategy. *Science, 275*(5304), 1293-1295.

Berthoz, S., & Hill, E. L. (2005). The validity of using self-reports to assess emotion regulation abilities in adults with autism spectrum disorder. *European Psychiatry, 20*(3), 291-298.

Bird, G., & Cook, R. (2013). Mixed emotions: the contribution of alexithymia to the emotional symptoms of autism. *Translational Psychiatry, 3*(7), e285.

Bird, G., Silani, G., Brindley, R., White, S., Frith, U., & Singer, T. (2010). Empathic brain responses in insula are modulated by levels of alexithymia but not autism. *Brain, 133*(5), 1515-1525.

Cascio, C., McGlone, F., Folger, S., Tannan, V., Baranek, G., Pelphrey, K.A., & Essick, G. (2008). Tactile perception in adults with autism: A multidimensional psychophysical study. *J. Autism Dev. Disord, 38,* 127–137.

Cook, R., Brewer, R., Shah, P., & Bird, G. (2013). Alexithymia, not autism, predicts poor recognition of emotional facial expressions. *Psychological Science, 24*(5), 723.

Craig, A. D. (2014). *How do you feel? An interoceptive moment with your neurobiological self.* Princeton, NJ: Princeton University Press.

Craig, A. D. (2009). How do you feel – Now? The anterior insula and human awareness. *Nature Reviews Neuroscience, 10*(1).

Craig, A. D. (2003). Interoception: The sense of the physiological condition of the body. *Current Opinion in Neurobiology, 13*(4), 500-505.

Craig, A. D. (2002). How do you feel? Interoception: The sense of the physiological condition of the body. *Nature Reviews Neuroscience, 3*(8), 655-666.

Critchley, H. D. (2005). Neural mechanisms of autonomic, affective, and cognitive integration. *Journal of Comparative Neurology, 493*(1), 154-166.

Critchley, H. D., Wiens, S., Rotshtein, P., Öhman, A., & Dolan, R. J. (2004). Neural systems supporting interoceptive awareness. *Nature Neuroscience, 7*(2), 189-195.

Damasio, A. (2010). *Self comes to mind: Constructing the conscious brain.* New York, NY: William Heinemann.

Damasio, A. R. (1996). The somatic marker hypothesis and the possible functions of the prefrontal cortex. *Phil Trans R Soc Lond B, 351*, 413-1420.

Damasio, A. R. (1994). *Descartes' error: Emotion, reason, and the human brain.* New York, NY: Grosset/Putnam.

Daubenmier, J., Sze, J., Kerr, C. E., Kemeny, M. E., & Mehling, W. (2013). Follow your breath: Respiratory interoceptive accuracy in experienced meditators. *Psychophysiology, 50*(8), 777-789.

De Martino, B., Harrison, N. A., Knafo, S., Bird, G., & Dolan, R. J. (2008). Explaining enhanced logical consistency during decision-making in autism. *The Journal of Neuroscience, 28*(42), 10746-10750.

Demiralp, E., Thompson, R. J., Mata, J., Jaeggi, S. M., Buschkuehl, M., Barrett, L. F., ... & Jonides, J. (2012). Feeling blue or turquoise? Emotional differentiation in major depressive disorder. *Psychological Science, 23*(11), 1410-1416.

Dickstein, D. P., Pescosolido, M. F., Reidy, B. L., Galvan, T., Kim, K. L., Seymour, K. E., ... & Barrett, R. P. (2013). Developmental meta-analysis of the functional neural correlates of autism spectrum disorders. *Journal of the American Academy of Child & Adolescent Psychiatry, 52*(3), 279-289.

DiMartino, A., Yan, C. G., Li, Q., Denio, E., Castellanos, F. X., Alaerts, K., ... & Milham, M. P. (2014). The autism brain imaging data exchange: Towards a large-scale evaluation of the intrinsic brain architecture in autism. *Molecular Psychiatry, 19*(6), 659-667.

DiMartino, A., Ross K., Uddin L., Sklar A., Costellanos, F. X. (2009). Functional brain correlates of social and nonsocial processes in autism spectrum disorders: An activation likelihood estimation meta-analysis. *Biological Psychiatry, 65*, 63-74.

Dunn, B. D., Galton, H. C., Morgan, R., Evans, D., Oliver, C., Meyer, M., ... & Dalgleish, T. (2010). Listening to your heart: How interoception shapes emotion experience and intuitive decision making. *Psychological Science, 21*(12), 1835-1844.

Dunn, W., Myles, B. S., & Orr, S. (2002). Sensory processing issues associated with Asperger syndrome: A preliminary investigation. *American Journal of Occupational Therapy, 56*(1), 97-102.

Erbas, Y., Ceulemans, E., Boonen, J., Noens, I., & Kuppens, P. (2013). Emotion differentiation in autism spectrum disorder. *Research in Autism Spectrum Disorders, 7*(10), 1221-1227.

Erbas, Y., Ceulemans, E., Lee Pe, M., Koval, P., & Kuppens, P. (2014). Negative emotion differentiation: Its personality and well-being correlates and a comparison of different assessment methods. *Cognition and Emotion, 28*(7), 1196-1213.

Evans, J. (2003). In two minds: Dual-process accounts of reasoning. *Trends in Cognitive Sciences, 7*(10), 454-459.

Farb, N. A., Anderson, A. K., Mayberg, H., Bean, J., McKeon, D., & Segal, Z. V. (2010). Minding one's emotions: Mindfulness training alters the neural expression of sadness. *Emotion, 10*(1), 25.

Farb, N. A., Segal, Z. V., Mayberg, H., Bean, J., McKeon, D., Fatima, Z., & Anderson, A. K. (2007). Attending to the present: Mindfulness meditation reveals distinct neural modes of self-reference. *Social Cognitive and Affective Neuroscience, 2*(4), 313-322.

Fiene, L., & Brownlow, C. (2015). Investigating interoception and body awareness in adults with and without autism spectrum disorder. *Autism Research.* doi:10.1002/aur.1486

Fuchs, T., & Koch, S. C. (2014). Embodied affectivity: On moving and being moved. *Frontiers in Psychology, 5*, 508. doi:10.3389/fpsyg.2014.00508

Füstös, J., Gramann, K., Herbert, B. M., & Pollatos, O. (2012). On the embodiment of emotion regulation: Interoceptive awareness facilitates reappraisal. *Social Cognitive and Affective Neuroscience*, nss089.

Gladwell, M. (2007). *Blink: The power of thinking without thinking.* New York, NY: Back Bay Books.

Gross, J. J. (1998). The emerging field of emotion regulation: An integrative review. *Review of General Psychology, 2*(3), 271.

Grossman, P., Niemann, L., Schmidt, S., & Walach, H. (2004). Mindfulness-based stress reduction and health benefits: A meta-analysis. *Journal of Psychosomatic Research, 57*(1), 35-43.

Grynberg, D., & Pollatos, O. (2015). Perceiving one's body shapes empathy. *Physiology and Behavior, 140*, 54-60.

Gu, X., Eilam-Stock, T., Zhou, T., Anagnostou, E., Kolevzon, A., Soorya, L., ... & Fan, J. (2015). Autonomic and brain responses associated with empathy deficits in autism spectrum disorder. *Human Brain Mapping*.

Gu, X., Wang, X., Hula, A., Wang, S., Xu, S., Lohrenz, T. M., ... & Montague, P. R. (2015). Necessary, yet dissociable contributions of the insular and ventromedial prefrontal cortices to norm adaptation: Computational and lesion evidence in humans. *The Journal of Neuroscience, 35*(2), 467-473.

Gu, X., & Fitzgerald, T. H. (2014). Interoceptive inference: Homeostasis and decision-making. *Trends Cognitive Science, 18*(6), 269-270.

Gu, X., Hof, P. R., Friston, K. J., & Fan, J. (2013). Anterior insular cortex and emotional awareness. *The Journal of Comparative Neurology, 521*(15), 3371-3388. doi:10.1002/cne.23368

Gu, X., Liu, X., Van Dam, N. T., Hof, P. R., & Fan, J. (2013). Cognition-emotion integration in the anterior insular cortex. *Cerebral Cortex, 23*(1), 20-27.

Gu, X., Gao, Z., Wang, X., Liu, X., Knight, R. T., Hof, P. R., & Fan, J. (2012). Anterior insular cortex is necessary for empathetic pain perception. *Brain, 135*(9), 2726-2735.

Herbert, B. M., & Pollatos, O. (2012). The body in the mind: On the relationship between interoception and embodiment. *Topics in Cognitive Science, 4*(4), 692-704.

Herbert, B. M., Herbert, C., & Pollatos, O. (2011). On the relationship between interoceptive awareness and alexithymia: Is interoceptive awareness related to emotional awareness? *Journal of Personality, 79*(5), 1149-1175.

Herbert, B. M., Pollatos, O., & Schandry, R. (2007). Interoceptive sensitivity and emotion processing: An EEG study. *International Journal of Psychophysiology, 65*(3), 214-227.

Hill, E., Berthoz, S., & Frith, U. (2004). Brief report: Cognitive processing of own emotions in individuals with autistic spectrum disorder and in their relatives. *Journal of Autism and Developmental Disorders, 34*(2), 229-235.

Hölzel, B. K., Carmody, J., Vangel, M., Congleton, C., Yerramsetti, S. M., Gard, T., & Lazar, S. W. (2011). Mindfulness practice leads to increases in regional brain gray matter density. *Psychiatry Research: Neuroimaging, 191*(1), 36-43.

Hölzel, B. K., Ott, U., Gard, T., Hempel, H., Weygandt, M., Morgen, K., & Vaitl, D. (2008). Investigation of mindfulness meditation practitioners with voxel-based morphometry. *Social Cognitive and Affective Neuroscience, 3*(1), 55-61.

Jackson, S. R., Parkinson, A., Kim, S. Y., Schüermann, M., & Eickhoff, S. B. (2011). On the functional anatomy of the urge-for-action. *Cognitive Neuroscience, 2*(3-4), 227-243.

Jahromi, L. B., Meek, S. E., & Ober-Reynolds, S. (2012). Emotion regulation in the context of frustration in children with high functioning autism and their typical peers. *Journal of Child Psychology and Psychiatry, 53*(12), 1250-1258.

James, W. (1884). What is an emotion? *Mind, 34,* 188-205.

Kabat-Zinn, J. (1994). *Wherever you go, there you are.* New York, NY: Hyperion.

Kahneman, D. (2003). Maps of bounded rationality: Psychology for behavioral economics. *American Economic Review,* 1449-1475.

Kanner, L. (1943). Autistic disturbances of affective contact. *Nervous Child, 2,* 217-250.

Kapp, S. K. (2013). Empathizing with sensory and movement differences: moving toward sensitive understanding of autism. *Frontiers in Integrative Neuroscience, 7,* 38.

Kashdan, T. B., & Farmer, A. S. (2014). Differentiating emotions across contexts: Comparing adults with and without social anxiety disorder using random, social interaction, and daily experience sampling. *Emotion, 14*(3), 629.

Kashdan, T. B., Ferssizidis, P., Collins, R. L., & Muraven, M. (2010). Emotion differentiation as resilience against excessive alcohol use: An ecological momentary assessment in underage social drinkers. *Psychological Science, 21*(9), 1341-1347.

Khalsa, S. S., Rudrauf, D., Damasio, A. R., Davidson, R. J., Lutz, A., & Tranel, D. (2008). Interoceptive awareness in experienced meditators. *Psychophysiology, 45*(4), 671-677.

Klin, A., & Volkmar, F. R. (1997). The pervasive developmental disorders: Nosology and profiles of development. In S. S. Luthar (Ed.), *Developmental psychopathology: Perspectives on adjustment, risk, and disorder* (pp. 208-226). Cambridge, England: Cambridge University Press.

Kopp, C. B. (1982). Antecedents of self-regulation: A developmental perspective. *Developmental Psychology, 18*(2), 199.

Kurth, F., Zilles, K., Fox, P. T., Laird, A. R., & Eickhoff, S. B. (2010). A link between the systems: Functional differentiation and integration within the human insula revealed by meta-analysis. *Brain Structure and Function, 214*(5-6), 519-534.

Lakoff, G., & Johnson, M. (1980). Conceptual metaphor in everyday language. *The Journal of Philosophy,* 453-486.

Lambie, J. A., & Marcel, A. J. (2002). Consciousness and the varieties of emotion experience: A theoretical framework. *Psychological Review, 109*(2), 219.

Lamm, C., & Singer, T. (2010). The role of anterior insular cortex in social emotions. *Brain Structure and Function, 214*(5-6), 579-591.

Lane, R. D., Sechrest, L., Riedel, R., Shapiro, D. E., & Kaszniak, A. W. (2000). Pervasive emotion recognition deficit common to alexithymia and the repressive coping style. *Psychosomatic Medicine, 62*(4), 492-501.

Lane, R. D., & Schwartz, G. E. (1987). Levels of emotional awareness: A cognitive-developmental theory and its application to psychopathology. *The American Journal of Psychiatry, 144*(2), 133-43.

Laurent, A. C. & Rubin, E. (2004). Emotional regulation challenges in Asperger's syndrome and high functioning autism. *Topics in Language Disorders, 24*, 4.

Lazar, S. W., Kerr, C. E., Wasserman, R. H., Gray, J. R., Greve, D. N., Treadway, M. T., ... Fischl, B. (2005). Meditation experience is associated with increased cortical thickness. *Neuroreport, 16*(17), 1893-1897.

Lutz, A., Slagter, H. A., Dunne, J. D., & Davidson, R. J. (2008). Attention regulation and monitoring in meditation. *Trends in Cognitive Sciences, 12*(4), 163-169. doi:10.1016/j.tics.2008.01.005

Mazefsky, C. A., Borue, X., Day, T. N., & Minshew, N. J. (2014). Emotion regulation patterns in adolescents with high-functioning autism spectrum disorder: Comparison to typically developing adolescents and association with psychiatric symptoms. *Autism Research, 7*(3), 344-354.

Mazefsky, C. A., & White, S. W. (2014). Emotion regulation: Concepts and practice in autism spectrum disorder. *Child and Adolescent Psychiatric Clinics of North America, 23*(1), 15-24.

Mazefsky, C. A., Herrington, J., Siegel, M., Scarpa, A., Maddox, B. B., Scahill, L., & White, S. W. (2013). The role of emotion regulation in autism spectrum disorder. *Journal of the American Academy of Child & Adolescent Psychiatry, 52*(7), 679-688.

McGlone, F., Wessberg, J., & Olausson, H. (2014). Discriminative and affective touch: Sensing and feeling. *Neuron, 82*(4), 737-755.

Mehling, W. E., Price, C., Daubenmier, J. J., Acree, M., Bartmess, E., & Stewart, A. (2012). The multidimensional assessment of interoceptive awareness (MAIA). PLoS One, 7(11), e48230. doi:10.1371/journal.pone.0048230

Mehling, W. E., Gopisetty, V., Daubenmier, J., Price, C. J., Hecht, F. M., & Stewart, A. (2009). Body awareness: Construct and self-report measures. *PLoS ONE, 4*(5), e5614. doi:10.1371/journal.pone.0005614

Menon, V., & Uddin, L. Q. (2010). Saliency, switching, attention and control: A network model of insula function. *Brain Structure and Function, 214*(5-6), 655-667.

Modinos, G., Ormel, J., & Aleman, A. (2009). Activation of anterior insula during self-reflection. *PLoS One, 4*(2), e4618-e4618.

Myles, B. S., & Aspy, R. (2016). *High-functioning autism and difficult moments: Practical solutions for reducing meltdowns.* Shawnee Mission, KS: AAPC Publishing.

Myles, B. S., Mahler, K., & Robbins, L. A. (2014). *Sensory issues and high-functioning autism spectrum and related disorders: Practical solutions for making sense of the world* (2nd ed.). Shawnee Mission, KS: AAPC Publishing.

Myles, B. S., Endow, J., & Mayfield, M. (2013). *The hidden curriculum of getting and keeping a job: Navigating the social landscape of employment.* Shawnee Mission, KS: AAPC Publishing.

Myles, H. M., & Kolar, A. (2013). *The hidden curriculum and other everyday challenges for elementary-age children with high-functioning autism.* Shawnee Mission, KS: AAPC Publishing.

Myles, B. S., Trautman, M. L., & Schelvan, R. L. (2013). *The hidden curriculum for understanding unstated rules in social situations for adolescents and young adults* (2nd ed.). Shawnee Mission, KS: AAPC Publishing.

Myles, B. S. (2003). Behavioral forms of stress management for individuals with Asperger syndrome. *Child and Adolescent Psychiatric Clinics of North America, 12*(1), 123-141.

Naidich, T. P., Kang, E., Fatterpekar, G. M., Delman, B. N., Gultekin, S. H., Wolfe, D., ... & Yousry, T. A. (2004). The insula: Anatomic study and MR imaging display at 1.5 T. *American Journal of Neuroradiology, 25*(2), 222-232.

Nomi, J. S., & Uddin, L. Q. (2015). Developmental changes in large-scale network connectivity in autism. *NeuroImage: Clinical, 7,* 732-741.

Olausson, H., Wessberg, J., McGlone, F., & Vallbo, Å. (2010). The neurophysiology of unmyelinated tactile afferents. *Neuroscience & Biobehavioral Reviews, 34*(2), 185-191.

Olausson, H., Lamarre, Y., Backlund, H., Morin, C., Wallin, B. G., Starck, G., ... & Bushnell, M. C. (2002). Unmyelinated tactile afferents signal touch and project to insular cortex. *Nature Neuroscience, 5*(9), 900-904.

Paulus, M. P., & Stein, M. B. (2010). Interoception in anxiety and depression. *Brain Structure and Function, 214*(5-6), 451-463.

Pollatos, O., Gramann, K., & Schandry, R. (2007). Neural systems connecting interoceptive awareness and feelings. *Human Brain Mapping, 28*(1), 9-18.

Pollatos, O., Kirsch,W., & Schandry, R. (2005). On the relationship between interoceptive awareness, emotional experience, and brain processes. *Cognitive Brain Research, 25*(3), 948-962.

Pond, R. S., Kashdan, T. B., DeWall, C. N., Savostyanova, A., Lambert, N. M., & Fincham, F. D. (2012). Emotion differentiation moderates aggressive tendencies in angry people: A daily diary analysis. *Emotion, 12*(2), 326.

Radeloff, D., Ciaramidaro, A., Siniatchkin, M., Hainz, D., Schlitt, S., Weber, B., ... & Freitag, C. M. (2014). Structural alterations of the social brain: A comparison between schizophrenia and autism. *PloS One, 9*(9), e106539.

Rieffe, C., Oosterveld, P., Terwogt, M. M., Mootz, S., van Leeuwen, E., & Stockmann, L. (2011). Emotion regulation and internalizing symptoms in children with autism spectrum disorders. *Autism, 15*(6), 655-670.

Rieffe, C., Oosterveld, P., & Meerum Terwogt, M. (2006). An alexithymia questionnaire for children: Factorial and concurrent validation results. *Personality and Individual Differences, 40*, 123-133.

Samson, A. C., Hardan, A. Y., Podell, R. W., Phillips, J. M., & Gross, J. J. (2015). Emotion regulation in children and adolescents with autism spectrum disorder. *Autism Research, 8*(1), 9-18.

Samson, A. C., Phillips, J. M., Parker, K. J., Shah, S., Gross, J. J., & Hardan, A. Y. (2014). Emotion dysregulation and the core features of autism spectrum disorder. *Journal of Autism and Developmental Disorders, 44*(7), 1766-1772.

Samson, A. C., Huber, O., & Gross, J. J. (2012). Emotion regulation in Asperger's syndrome and high-functioning autism. *Emotion, 12*(4), 659.

Sanfey, A. G., Rilling, J. K., Aronson, J. A., Nystrom, L. E., & Cohen, J. D. (2003). The neural basis of economic decision-making in the ultimatum game. *Science, 300*(5626), 1755-1758.

Seth, A. K. (2013). Interoceptive inference, emotion, and the embodied self. *Trends in Cognitive Sciences, 17*(11), 565-573.

Shields, S. A., Mallory, M. E., & Simon, A. (1989). The body awareness questionnaire: Reliability and validity. *Journal of Personality Assessment, 53*(4), 802-815.

Sherrington, C. S. (1906). *The integrative action of the nervous system*. New Haven, CT: Yale University Press.

Silani, G., Bird, G., Brindley, R., Singer, T., Frith, C., & Frith, U. (2008). Levels of emotional awareness and autism: An fMRI study. *Social Neuroscience, 3*(2), 97-112.

Singer, T., Seymour, B., O'Doherty, J., Kaube, H., Dolan, R. J., & Frith, C. D. (2004). Empathy for pain involves the affective but not sensory components of pain. *Science, 303*(5661), 1157-1162.

Tomchek, S. D., & Dunn, W. (2007). Sensory processing in children with and without autism: A comparative study using the short sensory profile. *American Journal of Occupational Therapy, 61*(2), 190-200.

Tsakiris, M., Hesse, M. D., Boy, C., Haggard, P., & Fink, G. R. (2007). Neural signatures of body ownership: A sensory network for bodily self-consciousness. *Cerebral Cortex, 17*(10), 2235-2244.

Tugade, M. M., Fredrickson, B. L., & Feldman Barrett, L. (2004). Psychological resilience and positive emotional granularity: Examining the benefits of positive emotions on coping and health. *Journal of Personality, 72*(6), 1161-1190.

Uddin, L. Q. (2015). Salience processing and insular cortical function and dysfunction. *Nature Reviews Neuroscience, 16*(1), 55-61.

Uddin, L. Q., Supekar, K., Lynch, C. J., Cheng, K. M., Odriozola, P., Barth, M. E., ... & Menon, V. (2014). Brain state differentiation and behavioral flexibility in autism. *Cerebral Cortex.* doi:10.1093/cercor.bhul61.

Uddin, L. Q., Supekar, K., & Menon, V. (2013). Reconceptualizing functional brain connectivity in autism from a developmental perspective. *Frontiers in Human Neuroscience, 7.*

Uddin, L. Q., Supekar, K., Lynch, C. J., Khouzam, A., Phillips, J., Feinstein, C., ... & Menon, V. (2013). Salience network-based classification and prediction of symptom severity in children with autism. *JAMA Psychiatry, 70*(8), 869-879.

Uljarevic, M., & Hamilton, A. (2013). Recognition of emotions in autism: A formal meta-analysis. *Journal of Autism and Developmental Disorders, 43*(7), 1517-1526.

Vermeulen, P. (2012). *Autism as context blindness.* Shawnee Mission, KS: AAPC Publishing.

Werner, N. S., Jung, K., Duschek, S., & Schandry, R. (2009). Enhanced cardiac perception is associated with benefits in decision-making. *Psychophysiology, 46*(6), 1123-1129.

Wiens, S. (2005). Interoception in emotional experience. *Current Opinion in Neurology, 18*(4), 442-447.

Xiang, T., Lohrenz, T., & Montague, P. R. (2013). Computational substrates of norms and their violations during social exchange. *The Journal of Neuroscience, 33*(3), 1099-1108.

The Interoceptive Awareness Interview

To Administer: Read each Main Question aloud and record the individual's answer in the space provided. If an individual has difficulty answering the Main Question, refer to the suggested Follow-Up Questions or Prompts in an effort to maximize the amount of information shared.

Question	Answer
1. **Main Question**: Do you ever feel stressed?	
2. **Main Question**: If so, how often? **Follow-up Questions or Prompts:** Do you feel stressed every day? Multiple times per day? All of the time?	
3. **Main Question**: What are a few things that typically make you feel stressed? **Follow-up Questions or Prompts**: Name as many as possible. What else makes you feel stressed? Are you ever unsure about why you are stressed?	

4. **Main Question:** How does your body feel when you are stressed? **Follow-up Questions or Prompts:** Name as many changes/symptoms as possible. Does your body feel different when you are stressed? How do you know when you are stressed?	
5. **Main Question**: What are some things you do to de-stress/calm down/relax? **Follow-up Questions or Prompts:** Name as many as possible. What else do you do? What do you do when you are stressed?	
6. **Main Question**: Is _____(insert strategy from above) effective? **Follow-up Questions or Prompts:** Does_____(strategy) work? Why or why not?	
7. **Main Question:** How does your body feel when you are angry? **Follow-up Questions or Prompts:** Name as many changes as possible. Does your body feel different when you are angry? How do you know when you are angry?	

8. **Main Question:** Does your body feel different when you are a little angry vs. really angry? Describe. **Follow-up Questions or Prompts:** If the individual cannot answer this question, but reports that the strategies identified in question 6 are effective, ask: How do you know when to use_____(insert strategy)? What gives you a clue?	
9. **Main Question:** How does your body feel when you are nervous? **Follow-up Questions or Prompts:** Name as many changes as possible. Does your body feel different when you are nervous? How do you know when you are nervous?	
10. **Main Question:** Do you ever feel embarrassed? How does your body feel when you are embarrassed? **Follow-up Questions or Prompts:** Name as many changes as possible. Does your body feel different when you are embarrassed? How do you know when you are embarrassed?	

From *Interoception: The Eighth Sensory System* by K. Mahler. Copyright 2016. Shawnee Mission, KS: AAPC Publishing.

11. **Main Question:** How does your body feel when you are calm or relaxed? **Follow-up Questions or Prompts:** Name as many changes as possible. Do you ever feel completely calm or relaxed? Does your body feel different when you are calm or relaxed? How do you know when you are calm or relaxed?	
12. **Main Question:** Do you notice a change in the way your body feels when you are tired and need sleep? **Follow-up Questions or Prompts:** How do you know when you need to go to bed? Do you go to bed at the same time each night? How do you feel when you are falling asleep?	
13. **Main Question:** How does your body feel when you are hungry? **Follow-up Questions or Prompts:** Name as many changes as possible. Does your body feel different when you are hungry?	
14. **Main Question:** Do you ever think you are hungry, get a snack, and then can't eat it? If yes, describe. **Follow-up Questions or Prompts:** Does this happen often?	

15. **Main Question:** Do you ever eat a large amount of food and not feel full? **Follow-up Questions or Prompts:** Do you ever eat too much, to the point of getting sick? Does this happen often? How does your body feel when you are full?	
16. **Main Question:** What does your body feel like when you are thirsty? **Follow-up Questions or Prompts:** Name as many changes as possible. Does your body feel different when you are thirsty? How do you know when you are thirsty? Do you ever go for really long periods without a drink?	
17. **Main Question:** Do you notice changes in the way your body feels when you need to go to the bathroom? If so, describe. **Follow-up Questions or Prompts:** How do you know when it is time to go to the bathroom?	
18. **Main Question:** Have you ever been injured and did not feel pain? If so, describe. **Follow-up Questions or Prompts:** Do you have a really high/low pain tolerance?	

From *Interoception: The Eighth Sensory System* by K. Mahler. Copyright 2016. Shawnee Mission, KS: AAPC Publishing.

19. **Main Question**: How do you know when your body has had enough physical activity? **Follow-up Questions or Prompts:** How do you know your body needs a break when you are active (e.g., playing a sport)? Do you ever over-do physical activity? Describe.	
20. **Main Question**: Can you tell when you have a fever without using a thermometer? If so, how do you know? **Follow-up Questions or Prompts:** Do you feel different when you have a fever? Does your body change?	
21. **Main Question**: Have you ever been sick and not realized it (e.g., had strep throat for a few days before you realized it)?	
22. **Main Question**: Do big emotions tend to sneak up on you? **Follow-up Questions or Prompts:** Do you feel both small emotions and really big emotions? Do you ever get really, really angry and not know why?	

Blank protocols are available from www.aapcpublishing.net. Look for *The Comprehensive Assessment for Interoceptive Awareness.*

From *Interoception: The Eighth Sensory System* by K. Mahler. Copyright 2016. Shawnee Mission, KS: AAPC Publishing.

The Assessment of Self-Regulation

Sample Questions

To Administer: Show the individual the first picture and ask the first question listed. No clues or prompts should be given. Record the answer in the space provided. Continue by asking the second question and record the answer in the corresponding space. At this point, if the individual did not identify the body state/emotion and cause accurately, provide the correct answer to Questions 1 & 2 (e.g., "She is nervous because she is about to perform onstage"). Once the correct answers are provided, proceed with the remaining questions and record the answers in the spaces provided. Do not provide answers for any of the remaining questions. After all pictures are completed, transfer scores from each individual picture to the master score sheet provided. Use this sheet to tally the score.

Question	Answer	Points
How does this person feel? 1 point = correct answer 0 points = incorrect answer or vague answer like "bad" or "OK"		/1
What is making him feel that way? 1 point = correct answer 0 points = incorrect answer		/1
What makes you feel excited? Give at least three examples. 1 point for each reasonable answer		/3
When you are excited, how does your body feel? Give at least three examples. 1 point for each reasonable answer		/3
If you were in this situation, what would you do to feel better? Give at least three examples.	No solution is needed for a positive situation and emotion.	
	TOTAL	/8

Question	Answer	Points
How does this person feel? 1 point = correct answer 0 points = incorrect answer or vague answer like "bad" or "OK"		/1
What is making her feel that way? 1 point = correct answer 0 points = incorrect answer		/1
What makes you feel nervous? Give at least three examples. 1 point for each reasonable answer		/3
When you are nervous, how does your body feel? Give at least three examples. 1 point for each reasonable answer		/3
If you were in this situation, what would you do to feel better? Give at least three examples. 1 point = for each detailed answer 0 points = for general answers, such as just don't do it, just leave, just walk away		/3
	TOTAL	/11

Question	Answer	Points
How does this person feel? 1 point = correct answer 0 points = incorrect answer or vague answer like "bad" or "OK"		/1
What is making her feel that way? 1 point = correct answer 0 points = incorrect answer		/1
What makes you feel cold? Give at least three examples. 1 point for each reasonable answer		/3
When you are cold, how does your body feel? Give at least three examples. 1 point for each reasonable answer		/3
If you were in this situation, what would you do to feel better? Give at least three examples. 1 point = for each detailed answer 0 points = for general answers, such as just don't do it, just leave, just walk away		/3
	TOTAL	/11

Question	Answer	Points
How does this person feel? 1 point = correct answer 0 points = incorrect answer or vague answer like "bad" or "OK"		/1
What is making her feel that way? 1 point = correct answer 0 points = incorrect answer		/1
What makes you feel angry? Give at least three examples. 1 point for each reasonable answer		/3
When you are angry, how does your body feel? Give at least three examples. 1 point for each reasonable answer		/3
If you were in this situation, what would you do to feel better? Give at least three examples. 1 point = for each detailed answer 0 points = for general answers, such as just don't do it, just leave, just walk away		/3
	TOTAL	/11

From *Interoception: The Eighth Sensory System* by K. Mahler. Copyright 2016. Shawnee Mission, KS: AAPC Publishing.

Question	Answer	Points
How do these people feel? 1 point = correct answer 0 points = incorrect answer or vague answer "bad" or "OK"		/1
What is making them feel that way? 1 point = correct answer 0 points = incorrect answer		/1
What makes you feel happy? Give at least three examples. 1 point for each reasonable answer		/3
When you are happy, how does your body feel? Give at least three examples. 1 point for each reasonable answer		/3
If you were in this situation, what would you do to feel better? Give at least three examples.	No solution is needed for a positive situation and emotion.	
	TOTAL	/8

Question	Answer	Points
How does this person feel? 1 point = correct answer 0 points = incorrect answer or vague answer like "bad" or "OK"		/1
What is making him feel that way? 1 point = correct answer 0 points = incorrect answer		/1
What makes you feel sick? Give at least three examples. 1 point for each reasonable answer		/3
When you are sick, how does your body feel? Give at least three examples. 1 point for each reasonable answer		/3
If you were in this situation, what would you do to feel better? Give at least three examples. 1 point = for each detailed answer 0 points = for general answers, such as just don't do it, just leave, just walk away		/3
	TOTAL	/11

From *Interoception: The Eighth Sensory System* by K. Mahler. Copyright 2016. Shawnee Mission, KS: AAPC Publishing.

Question	Answer	Points
How does this person feel? 1 point = correct answer 0 points = incorrect answer or vague answer like "bad" or "OK"		/1
What is making him feel that way? 1 point = correct answer 0 points = incorrect answer		/1
What makes you feel exhausted/hot? Give at least three examples. 1 point for each reasonable answer		/3
When you are exhausted/hot, how does your body feel? Give at least three examples. 1 point for each reasonable answer		/3
If you were in this situation, what would you do to feel better? Give at least three examples. 1 point = for each detailed answer 0 points = for general answers, such as just don't do it, just leave, just walk away		/3
	TOTAL	/11

Question	Answer	Points
How does the girl on the right feel? 1 point = correct answer 0 points = incorrect answer or vague answer like "bad" or "OK"		/1
What is making her feel that way? 1 point = correct answer 0 points = incorrect answer		/1
What makes you feel sad or left out? Give at least three examples. 1 point for each reasonable answer		/3
When you are sad/left out, how does your body feel? Give at least three examples. 1 point for each reasonable answer		/3
If you were in this situation, what would you do to feel better? Give at least three examples. 1 point = for each detailed answer 0 points = for general answers, such as just don't do it, just leave, just walk away		/3
	TOTAL	/11

From *Interoception: The Eighth Sensory System* by K. Mahler. Copyright 2016. Shawnee Mission, KS: AAPC Publishing.

Question	Answer	Points
How does this person feel? 1 point = correct answer 0 points = incorrect answer or vague answer like "bad" or "OK"		/1
What is making him feel that way? 1 point = correct answer 0 points = incorrect answer		/1
What makes you feel hurt? Give at least three examples. 1 point for each reasonable answer		/3
When you are hurt, how does your body feel? Give at least three examples. 1 point for each reasonable answer		/3
If you were in this situation, what would you do to feel better? Give at least three examples. 1 point = for each detailed answer 0 points = for general answers, such as just don't do it, just leave, just walk away		/3
	TOTAL	/11

Question	Answer	Points
How does this person feel? 1 point = correct answer 0 points = incorrect answer or vague answer like "bad" or "OK"		/1
What is making her feel that way? 1 point = correct answer 0 points = incorrect answer		/1
What makes you feel bored? Give at least three examples. 1 point for each reasonable answer		/3
When you are bored, how does your body feel? Give at least three examples. 1 point for each reasonable answer		/3
If you were in this situation, what would you do to feel better? Give at least three examples. 1 point = for each detailed answer 0 points = for general answers, such as just don't do it, just leave, just walk away		/3
	TOTAL	/11

Question	Answer	Points
How does this person feel? 1 point = correct answer 0 points = incorrect answer or vague answer like "bad" or "OK"		/1
What is making him feel that way? 1 point = correct answer 0 points = incorrect answer		/1
What makes you feel frustrated? Give at least three examples. 1 point for each reasonable answer		/3
When you are frustrated, how does your body feel? Give at least three examples. 1 point for each reasonable answer		/3
If you were in this situation, what would you do to feel better? Give at least three examples. 1 point = for each detailed answer 0 points = for general answers, such as just don't do it, just leave, just walk away		/3
	TOTAL	/11

Question	Answer	Points
How does this person feel? 1 point = correct answer 0 points = incorrect answer or vague answer like "bad" or "OK"		/1
What is making him feel that way? 1 point = correct answer 0 points = incorrect answer		/1
What makes you feel relaxed/ calm? Give at least three examples. 1 point for each reasonable answer		/3
When you are relaxed/calm, how does your body feel? Give at least three examples. 1 point for each reasonable answer		/3
If you were in this situation, what would you do to feel better? Give at least three examples.	No solution is needed for a positive situation and emotion.	
	TOTAL	/8

From *Interoception: The Eighth Sensory System* by K. Mahler. Copyright 2016. Shawnee Mission, KS: AAPC Publishing.

Question	Answer	Points
How does this person feel? 1 point = correct answer 0 points = incorrect answer or vague answer like "bad" or "OK"		/1
What is making her feel that way? 1 point = correct answer 0 points = incorrect answer		/1
What makes you feel worried? Give at least three examples. 1 point for each reasonable answer		/3
When you are worried, how does your body feel? Give at least three examples. 1 point for each reasonable answer		/3
If you were in this situation, what would you do to feel better? Give at least three examples. 1 point = for each detailed answer 0 points = for general answers, such as just don't do it, just leave, just walk away		/3
	TOTAL	/11

Question	Answer	Points
How does this person feel? 1 point = correct answer 0 points = incorrect answer or vague answer like "bad" or "OK"		/1
What is making her feel that way? 1 point = correct answer 0 points = incorrect answer		/1
What makes you feel surprised? Give at least three examples. 1 point for each reasonable answer		/3
When you are surprised, how does your body feel? Give at least three examples. 1 point for each reasonable answer		/3
If you were in this situation, what would you do to feel better? Give at least three examples.	No solution is needed for a positive situation and emotion	
	TOTAL	/8

From *Interoception: The Eighth Sensory System* by K. Mahler. Copyright 2016. Shawnee Mission, KS: AAPC Publishing.

Question	Answer	Points
How does this person feel? 1 point = correct answer 0 points = incorrect answer or vague answer like "bad" or "OK"		/1
What is making him feel that way? 1 point = correct answer 0 points = incorrect answer		/1
What makes you feel scared? Give at least three examples. 1 point for each reasonable answer		/3
When you are scared, how does your body feel? Give at least three examples. 1 point for each reasonable answer		/3
If you were in this situation, what would you do to feel better? Give at least three examples. 1 point = for each detailed answer 0 points = for general answers, such as just don't do it, just leave, just walk away		/3
TOTAL		/11

Question	Answer	Points
How does this woman feel? 1 point = correct answer 0 points = incorrect answer or vague answer like "bad" or "OK"		/1
What is making her feel that way? 1 point = correct answer 0 points = incorrect answer		/1
What makes you feel disgusted? Give at least three examples. 1 point for each reasonable answer		/3
When you are disgusted, how does your body feel? Give at least three examples. 1 point for each reasonable answer		/3
If you were in this situation, what would you do to feel better? Give at least three examples. 1 point = for each detailed answer 0 points = for general answers, such as just don't do it, just leave, just walk away		/3
	TOTAL	/11

From *Interoception: The Eighth Sensory System* by K. Mahler. Copyright 2016. Shawnee Mission, KS: AAPC Publishing.

Question	Answer	Points
How does this boy feel? 1 point = correct answer 0 points = incorrect answer or vague answer like "bad" or "OK"		/1
What is making him feel that way? 1 point = correct answer 0 points = incorrect answer		/1
What makes you feel embarrassed? Give at least three examples. 1 point for each reasonable answer		/3
When you are embarrassed, how does your body feel? Give at least three examples. 1 point for each reasonable answer		/3
If you were in this situation, what would you do to feel better? Give at least three examples. 1 point = for each detailed answer 0 points = for general answers, such as just don't do it, just leave, just walk away		/3
	TOTAL	/11

Question	Answer	Points
How does the girl on the right feel? 1 point = correct answer 0 points = incorrect answer or vague answer like "bad" or "OK"		/1
What is making her feel that way? 1 point = correct answer 0 points = incorrect answer		/1
What makes you feel jealous? Give at least three examples. 1 point for each reasonable answer		/3
When you are jealous, how does your body feel? Give at least three examples. 1 point for each reasonable answer		/3
If you were in this situation, what would you do to feel better? Give at least three examples. 1 point = for each detailed answer 0 points = for general answers, such as just don't do it, just leave, just walk away		/3
	TOTAL	/11

From *Interoception: The Eighth Sensory System* by K. Mahler. Copyright 2016. Shawnee Mission, KS: AAPC Publishing.

Master Score Sheet for Assessment of Self-Regulation

Directions: Calculate the scores from each picture and transfer to this master score sheet for total scores.

Question	Individual Scores		Total Points
Identifying Others' Body State or Emotion: How does this person feel?	Picture 1:_____ Picture 2:_____ Picture 3:_____ Picture 4:_____ Picture 5:_____ Picture 6:_____ Picture 7:_____ Picture 8:_____ Picture 9:_____	Picture 10:_____ Picture 11:_____ Picture 12:_____ Picture 13:_____ Picture 14:_____ Picture 15:_____ Picture 16:_____ Picture 17:_____ Picture 18:_____	Total Correct Points: ☐ ÷ Total Points Possible (1 point per picture used): ☐ = ☐%
Identifying Others' Causes or Triggers: What is making him feel that way?	Picture 1:_____ Picture 2:_____ Picture 3:_____ Picture 4:_____ Picture 5:_____ Picture 6:_____ Picture 7:_____ Picture 8:_____ Picture 9:_____	Picture 10:_____ Picture 11:_____ Picture 12:_____ Picture 13:_____ Picture 14:_____ Picture 15:_____ Picture 16:_____ Picture 17:_____ Picture 18:_____	Total Correct Points: ☐ ÷ Total Points Possible (1 point per picture used): ☐ = ☐%

From *Interoception: The Eighth Sensory System* by K. Mahler. Copyright 2016. Shawnee Mission, KS: AAPC Publishing.

Identifying Own Causes or Triggers: What makes you feel this way? Give at least three examples.	Picture 1:_____ Picture 10:_____ Picture 2:_____ Picture 11:_____ Picture 3:_____ Picture 12:_____ Picture 4:_____ Picture 13:_____ Picture 5:_____ Picture 14:_____ Picture 6:_____ Picture 15:_____ Picture 7:_____ Picture 16:_____ Picture 8:_____ Picture 17:_____ Picture 9:_____ Picture 18:_____	Total Correct Points: ☐ ÷ Total Points Possible (3 points per picture used): ☐ = ☐ %
Interoceptive Awareness: When you experience this body state/emotion, how does your body feel? Give at least three examples.	Picture 1:_____ Picture 10:_____ Picture 2:_____ Picture 11:_____ Picture 3:_____ Picture 12:_____ Picture 4:_____ Picture 13:_____ Picture 5:_____ Picture 14:_____ Picture 6:_____ Picture 15:_____ Picture 7:_____ Picture 16:_____ Picture 8:_____ Picture 17:_____ Picture 9:_____ Picture 18:_____	Total Correct Points: ☐ ÷ Total Points Possible (3 points per picture used): ☐ = ☐ %
Strategy Identification and Problem Solving: If you were in this situation, what would you do to feel better? Give at least three examples.	Picture 1: N/A Picture 10:_____ Picture 2:_____ Picture 11:_____ Picture 3:_____ Picture 12: N/A Picture 4:_____ Picture 13:_____ Picture 5: N/A Picture 14: N/A Picture 6:_____ Picture 15:_____ Picture 7:_____ Picture 16:_____ Picture 8:_____ Picture 17:_____ Picture 9:_____ Picture 18:_____	Total Correct Points: ☐ ÷ Total Points Possible (3 points per picture used): ☐ = ☐ %

From *Interoception: The Eighth Sensory System* by K. Mahler. Copyright 2016. Shawnee Mission, KS: AAPC Publishing.

The Caregiver Questionnaire for Interoceptive Awareness

Directions: Please read the following questions and provide the answer in the space provided.

Question	Answer
1. Does the individual have difficulty controlling emotions? If so, please explain what he tends to do when stressed.	
2. If the individual has difficulty controlling emotions, how often does this happen?	
3. What are a few things that typically make the individual stressed? Please share as many as possible.	
4. Does the individual use statements that identify how her body feels (e.g., my heart is pounding; my head is spinning)?	
5. What are some things the individual does to de-stress/calm down/relax?	
6. Are these strategies effective across settings? Explain.	
7. Is the individual able to discriminate between his emotions (e.g., feeling bored vs. tired)?	

8. Is the individual able to identify her basic emotions verbally (e.g., "I am frustrated" or "This is so sad")?	
9. Does the individual use a wide variety of emotion words when labeling how he feels (e.g., embarrassed, guilty, distracted, irritated)?	
10. Does the individual identify early emotions and react effectively (e.g., take a break when slightly frustrated rather than waiting until really angry)?	
11. Does the individual have periods where she appears completely relaxed or calm? Describe.	
12. Does the individual have difficulties with sleep? Describe.	
13. Does the individual report feeling hungry?	
14. Do you ever need to remind the individual to eat, even after long periods of time?	
15. Does the individual over-eat or eat to the point of getting sick?	
16. Do you ever need to remind the individual to drink? If yes, explain.	
17. Is the individual fully potty trained? Any accidents?	
18. Does the individual rush to the bathroom to avoid having an accident?	
19. Does the individual need to be reminded to use the bathroom, especially after long periods of time? If yes, explain.	

20. Does the individual experience frequent urinary or bowel issues (constipation, urinary tract infection, etc.)? If yes, explain.	
21. Has the individual ever been injured and not felt pain? If so, describe.	
22. Does the individual ever over-exert himself physically? If yes, explain.	
23. Does the individual ever report having a fever without using a thermometer?	
24. Has the individual ever been sick and not realized it (e.g., had strep throat for a few days before it was detected)?	

Blank protocols are available from www.aapcpublishing.net. Look for *The Comprehensive Assessment for Interoceptive Awareness.*

Adaptations for Reduced IA – Examples

Visual Supports

Go to the Bathroom At:
9:00
12:00
3:00

Remember to Eat at the Following Times:

7:30 - Breakfast

9:45 - Snack

12:00 - Lunch

3:30 - Snack

6:00 - Dinner

8:00 - Snack

Before I go to the playground, I put on the following items. These will help me feel warm when I am playing and having fun:

My Hat

My Vest

From *Interoception: The Eighth Sensory System* by K. Mahler. Copyright 2016. Shawnee Mission, KS: AAPC Publishing.
Used with permission.

Sample Social Narratives

Some people can tell when they hurt by the feelings in their body. For others, this can be a challenging thing to do. While you are learning the feelings IN your body, it is important to make sure that your body is okay. Every day before you shower, you need to do a mirror check.

Look at your body to see if there are any:

- Cuts
- Red spots
- Bruises
- Swollen or raised areas
- Anything with pus

If you see any of these, you need to immediately tell your mom or dad. This will help to keep you healthy.

It is healthy to empty your bladder a few times a day. Some people know when they have to go to the bathroom by the feelings in their body. Others may not have these feelings and do not empty their bladders frequently enough. Sometimes, this can lead to bladder infections or sometimes even an accident.

While you are learning about the feelings in my body, you need to make sure you are going to the bathroom several times a day. When you are at school, you need to try to use the bathroom at the following times:

9:00

12:00

3:00

Sometimes people have feelings in their body that tell them when they are starting to feel a little angry. These feelings help them to know that they need help or need to take a break. Other people do not have these feelings in their body that tell them when they are just a little bit angry. Sometimes they don't feel their anger until they are REALLY, REALLY angry. By then it is really tricky to ask for help or take a break.

While you are learning about the feelings in your body, your teacher/parent will use the following signal (created by student) to let you know when they see your anger just starting to rise. This will help you know when to ask for help or take a break before your anger gets too high.

IA Builders – Supplemental Materials

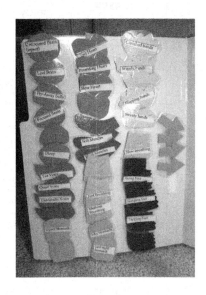

Suggested Body Areas for Body Check

Brain	Breathing
Eyes	Heart
Nose	Stomach
Cheeks	Muscles
Mouth/Jaw	Hands and fingers
Voice	Feet and toes
Ears	
Skin	*Or include your own!*

Suggested Descriptors for Each Body Part

These are merely suggestions. Incorporate the individual's descriptors whenever possible.

My Body Part (Body Part)	What I Feel (Descriptors)
Brain	Focused, distracted, dizzy, light-headed, tense, fast, swirly, heavy, blank, stuck, scattered
Eyes	Heavy, blurry, watery, stingy, itchy, squinty, teary
Nose	Runny, stuffy, tickly, itchy, burning
Cheeks	Warm, neutral, red, hot, tight, loose
Mouth/Jaw	Dry mouth, tight jaw, soft jaw, sore throat
Voice	Shut-off, loud, fast, slow, yelling, content
Ears	Focused, sensitive, bothered, shut-off, itchy, sore, distracted
Skin	Sweaty, itchy, goose bumps, bothered, tight, dry, content, OK
Breathing	Fast, slow, normal, tight, short, panting
Heart	Fast, slow, warm, swelling, full, pounding
Stomach	Content, hungry, full, fluttery, tingly, nauseous, heavy, gurgling
Muscles	Tense, tight, relaxed, normal, loose, heavy, sore, wiggly, antsy, bursting, hot, burning
Hands and fingers	Still, squeezing, moving, twisting, clenched, sweating, flapping, fidgeting
Feet and toes	Curling, wiggling, fidgeting, shaking, pacing, clenching, tapping, loose

Blank Body Outline

From *Interoception: The Eighth Sensory System* by K. Mahler. Copyright 2016. Shawnee Mission, KS: AAPC Publishing.
Used with permission.

IA Builder 2: IA on the Fly

Below are some suggested moments for when to pause and encourage the individual to attend to the internal body signals. Use the questions or create your own. This worksheet is only a guide. Find different opportunities and moments to pause and call attention to internal signals. The more frequently this activity happens, the faster an individual will become aware of the interoceptive system.

Tips:

- Encourage the individual to use detailed descriptors when attending to body sensations. Terms such as "hungry," "tired" and "fine" are vague and do not truly describe the related sensations (e.g., what does a hungry stomach feel like?).

- Begin with broad, general questions and, if needed to gain more information, follow up with a few specific questions.

- When first using IA on the Fly with an individual, it is good to focus on only one body part at a time to avoid overwhelm. Gradually build to attending to several body parts.

- In the beginning stages, remember to have a visual support nearby to guide this process (e.g., Body Check or a blank body outline).

Situation 1: At the completion of a physical activity (e.g., running on playground, playing tag, jogging a short distance, lifting weights), ask the individual to describe how one specific body part or a variety of body parts feel. Here are some suggested questions.

General Questions	Response
How does your body feel right now?	
Does your body feel any different after running/jumping/etc.? How so? What specifically changed?	

Specific Questions	Response
What do you notice about your heart rate? Put your hand over your chest and tell me what you feel.	
What do you notice about your breathing? Where do you feel your breathing change (nose, chest, etc.)? Describe how it feels.	
What do your muscles feel like after running/jumping/etc.?	
Did anything happen to your body temperature? How do you know? What does it feel like?	

Situation 2. Before it is time to eat a meal, especially after a long break from eating, ask the individual to describe how various body parts feel. Here are some suggested questions.

General Questions	Response
How does your body feel right now?	
It has been a long time since you ate. Does your body feel different? Do you notice any changes?	

Specific Questions	Response
How does your stomach feel right now? Describe. (Note: The answer, "hungry" does not count. Try to prompt the individual to describe the specific sensations; tingly, rumbling, etc.).	
How do your muscles feel?	
Any changes in your energy level? What does that feel like in your body?	
How does your brain feel?	

From *Interoception: The Eighth Sensory System* by K. Mahler. Copyright 2016. Shawnee Mission, KS: AAPC Publishing.
Used with permission.

Situation 3: In a moment when thirst would be highly possible (e.g., after physical exercise or on a hot day), ask the individual to describe how various body parts feel. Here are some suggested questions.

General Questions	Response
It has been a long time since you've had a drink. Does your body feel different? Do you notice any changes?	

Specific Questions	Response
How does your throat/mouth feel right now? Describe. (Note: The answer, "thirsty" does not count. Try to prompt the individual to describe the specific sensations.)	
How does you stomach feel?	
Any changes in your energy level? What does that feel like in your body?	

Situation 4: At bedtime, when the individual is visibly sleepy, ask her to describe how various body parts feel. Here are some suggested questions:

General Questions	Response
It is late and you have had a busy day. How does your body feel right now? Do you notice any changes?	

Specific Questions	Response
How do your eyes feel right now?	
How do your muscles feel?	
Any changes in your energy level? What does that feel like in your body?	
How does your brain feel?	
What do you notice in your voice?	

Situation 5: During a fun activity, when the individual is visibly excited, ask him to describe how various body parts feel. Here are some suggested questions:

General Questions	Response
How does your body feel right now?	
It looks like you are having a great time. What do you notice in your body?	

Specific Questions	Response
How does your heart feel right now?	
How do your muscles feel?	
Any changes in your energy level? What does that feel like in your body?	
How does your brain feel?	

IA Connector Form

Sensation 1	+	Sensation 2	+	Sensation 3	+	Sensation 4	=	Emotion/Body State
	+		+		+		=	
	+		+		+		=	
	+		+		+		=	

Suggested Stopping Points for Body Scan

Brain

Eyes

Nose

Cheeks

Mouth/Jaw

Voice

Ears

Skin

Breathing

Heart

Stomach

Muscles

Hands and fingers

Feet and toes

Body Scan – Instructor Guide

Body Part	Sample Descriptors	Sensation Reported by Individual
Brain	Focused, distracted, dizzy, light-headed, tense, fast, swirly, heavy, blank, stuck, scattered	Answer(s): Choices needed? Yes No
Eyes	Heavy, blurry, watery, stingy, itchy, squinty, teary	Answer(s): Choices needed? Yes No
Nose	Runny, stuffy, tickly, itchy, burning	Answer(s): Choices needed? Yes No
Cheeks	Warm, neutral, red, hot, tight, loose	Answer(s): Choices needed? Yes No
Mouth	Dry mouth, tight jaw, soft jaw, sore throat	Answer(s): Choices needed? Yes No
Voice	Shut-off, loud, fast, slow, yelling, content	Answer(s): Choices needed? Yes No
Ears	Focused, sensitive, bothered, shut-off, itchy, sore, distracted	Answer(s): Choices needed? Yes No
Skin	Sweaty, itchy, goose bumps, bothered, tight, dry, content, OK	Answer(s): Choices needed? Yes No
Breathing	Fast, slow, normal, tight, short, panting	Answer(s): Choices needed? Yes No
Heart	Fast, slow, warm, swelling, full, pounding	Answer(s): Choices needed? Yes No
Stomach	Content, hungry, full, fluttery, tingly, nauseous, heavy, gurgling	Answer(s): Choices needed? Yes No
Muscles	Tense, tight, relaxed, normal, loose, heavy, sore, wiggly, antsy, bursting, hot, burning	Answer(s): Choices needed? Yes No
Hands & fingers	Still, squeezing, moving, twisting, clenched, sweating, flapping, fidgeting	Answer(s): Choices needed? Yes No
Feet & toes	Curling, wiggling, fidgeting, shaking, pacing, clenching, tapping, loose	Answer(s): Choices needed? Yes No

Independent Body Scan – Sample

Adapt this form to include specific descriptions the individual uses.

Body Part	What I Feel (circle)
Brain	Focused, distracted, dizzy, light-headed, tense, fast, swirly, heavy, blank, stuck, scattered
Eyes	Heavy, blurry, watery, stingy, itchy, squinty, teary
Nose	Runny, stuffy, tickly, itchy, burning
Cheeks	Warm, neutral, red, hot, tight, loose
Mouth	Dry mouth, tight jaw, soft jaw, sore throat
Voice	Shut-off, loud, fast, slow, yelling, content
Ears	Focused, sensitive, bothered, shut-off, itchy, sore, distracted
Skin	Sweaty, itchy, goose bumps, bothered, tight, dry, content, OK
Breathing	Fast, slow, normal, tight, short, panting
Heart	Fast, slow, warm, swelling, full, pounding
Stomach	Content, hungry, full, fluttery, tingly, nauseous, heavy, gurgling
Muscles	Tense, tight, relaxed, normal, loose, heavy, sore, wiggly, antsy, bursting, hot, burning
Hands & fingers	Still, squeezing, moving, twisting, clenched, sweating, flapping, fidgeting
Feet & toes	Curling, wiggling, fidgeting, shaking, pacing, clenching, tapping, loose

From *Interoception: The Eighth Sensory System* by K. Mahler. Copyright 2016. Shawnee Mission, KS: AAPC Publishing.
Used with permission.

Independent Body Scan – Body Outline Guide

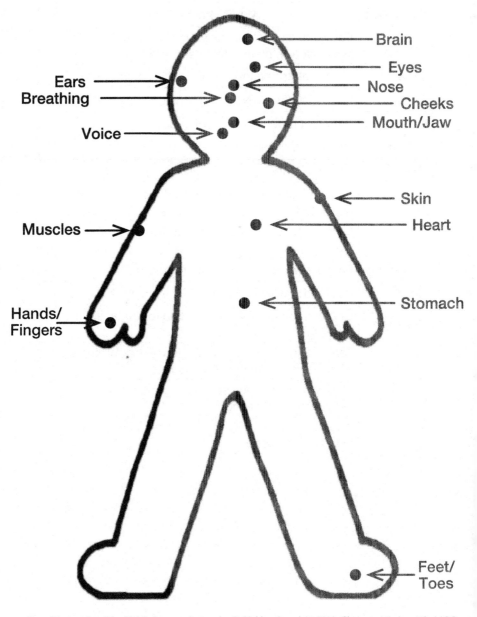

Brain

Eyes

Ears

Breathing

Nose

Cheeks

Mouth/Jaw

Voice

Skin

Muscles

Heart

Stomach

Hands/
Fingers

Feet/
Toes

Let It Out!

How Do the Following Body Areas Feel?

My Brain Feels:

My Eyes Feel:

My Nose Feels:

My Cheeks Feel:

My Mouth Feels:

My Voice Is:

My Ears Feel:

My Skin Feels:

My Breathing Feels:

My Heart Feels:

My Stomach Feels:

My Muscles Feel:

My Hands and Fingers Feel:

My Feet and Toes Feel:

From *Interoception: The Eighth Sensory System* by K. Mahler. Copyright 2016. Shawnee Mission, KS: AAPC Publishing.
Used with permission.

Let It Out! – Body Outline Guide

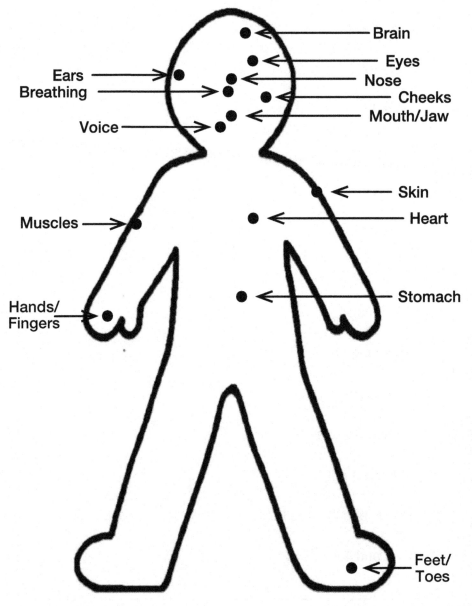

Brain

Eyes

Nose

Cheeks

Mouth/Jaw

Ears

Breathing

Voice

Skin

Heart

Muscles

Stomach

Hands/
Fingers

Feet/
Toes

Focus Area Activity Ideas

The following is a list of activities and experiences to explore. *Always* encourage focus on the various body sensations evoked by the activities and experiences. Although an activity might be listed under a specific body part (e.g., eyes), it is possible for sensations from other body parts to emerge. Use plenty of guiding questions and prompts, encourage critical thinking and avoid giving answers. Optional: Use a Body Check chart or body outline as a visual guide.

Note: Always be cognizant of sensory sensitivities and only proceed with an activity if the individual is comfortable.

Eyes
Explore different levels of lighting (e.g., dim lamp, bright sunlight, fluorescent lights, darkness, blinking lights)

Nose
Explore a variety of smells (e.g., mint, vanilla, lavender, citrus)

Cheeks
Put warm compress on cheeks and focus on sensations evoked

Mouth/Jaw
Eat a small sampling of a variety of foods (e.g., chewy, crunchy, cold, sour, minty, cinnamon, spicy)

Voice
Using a voice recorder, record student using a variety of tones of voice (e.g., yelling, whisper, silly voice)

Ears
Listen to a variety of sounds (e.g., slow music, fast music, loud music, nature sounds, quiet space, loud room, white noise)

Skin
Brush different areas of skin with a variety of textures (e.g., cotton ball, feather, sandpaper, deep touch massage, tickle, warm, cold)

Breathing
See IA Builder 11: Breathing Games
Use a variety of blow toys (e.g., whistles, bubbles, harmonica, blowing cotton ball with straw)

Heart
See IA Builders: Heartbeat Games; How Low Can you Go?; How Low Can you Go? – Advanced; Dueling Hearts

Stomach
At various points surrounding meals (e.g., before breakfast, after breakfast) compare feelings in stomach

Muscles
See IA Builder 12: Squeeze and Loosen

Hands and Fingers
Explore a variety of movements and fidgets (e.g., tapping fingers, squeezing stress ball, rubbing Velcro, stretching rubber band)

Feet and Toes
Explore a variety of movements (e.g., low jumping, high jumping, running, tapping)

Heartbeat Games

Activity	Heart Rate
At rest	
After 30 seconds of minimal activity	
After 1 minute of moderate activity	
After 2 minutes of intense activity	

Activity	Heart Rate
At rest	
After 30 seconds of minimal activity	
After 1 minute of moderate activity	
After 2 minutes of intense activity	

From *Interoception: The Eighth Sensory System* by K. Mahler. Copyright 2016. Shawnee Mission, KS: AAPC
Publishing.
Used with permission.

Heartbeat Games – Blank Log for Practice Opportunities

Activity	Heart Rate

Suggested Activity List

Minimal Activities:
- Walking in place
- Slow standing toe raises
- Slow chair push-ups
- Hand squeezes
- 1 yoga position (downward dog)
- Stretching
- Bouncing a tennis or basketball

Moderate Activities:
- Marching
- Slow jogging
- Slow bouncing on exercise ball
- Slow peddling on stationary or regular bike

Intense Activities:
- Running fast
- Riding stationary bike
- Jumping jacks
- Fast dancing
- Jumping (trampoline or in place)

From *Interoception: The Eighth Sensory System* by K. Mahler. Copyright 2016. Shawnee Mission, KS: AAPC Publishing.
Used with permission.

Guess Your Heart Rate!

Date	My Guess	Actual	Difference
March 10	125	100	25

How Low Can You Go?

Date	Starting Heart Rate	Ending Heart Rate	Difference	What Did I Do to Drop My Heart Rate?
June 18	114	84	30	Lay down, used even breathing, categorized animals in my mind

How Low Can You Go? – Advanced

Student Name	Starting Heart Rate	Ending Heart Rate	Difference
Ella	125	75	50

Dueling Hearts

Round 1:

Student 1 Name	Starting Heart Rate	Ending Heart Rate	Difference
Student 2 Name	Starting Heart Rate	Ending Heart Rate	Difference

Round 2:

Student 1 Name	Starting Heart Rate	Ending Heart Rate	Difference
Student 2 Name	Starting Heart Rate	Ending Heart Rate	Difference

Round 3:

Student 1 Name	Starting Heart Rate	Ending Heart Rate	Difference
Student 2 Name	Starting Heart Rate	Ending Heart Rate	Difference

From *Interoception: The Eighth Sensory System* by K. Mahler. Copyright 2016. Shawnee Mission, KS: AAPC Publishing.
Used with permission.

IA Builder 11: Breathing Games

Directions: *Complete the following activities using the amplifier. Then repeat without the use of the amplifier.*

Activity	Breathing Feels
At rest	
After 30 seconds of minimal activity	
After 1 minute of moderate activity	
After 2 minutes of intense activity	

Activity	Breathing Feels
At rest	
After 30 seconds of minimal activity	
After 1 minute of moderate activity	
After 2 minutes of intense activity	

IA Builder 12: Squeeze and Loosen

Pile 1 Cards:

Forehead	Hands	Toes
Cheeks	Lips	Jaw
Eyes	Shoulders	Arms
Legs	Nose	Back

Pile 2 Cards:

Squeeze	Loosen	Squeeze
Loosen	Squeeze	Loosen
Squeeze	Loosen	Squeeze
Loosen	Squeeze	Loosen

IA Builder 14: How Do I Feel? – Game Cards

Embarrassed	Cold	Hungry
Thirsty	Excited	Nervous
Calm	Scared	Hot

Supplemental materials are available for download at www.aapcpublishing.net/bookstore/books/9127.aspx.

Interoception Handout

Sit back and close your eyes. What do you feel *inside* your body?

- Is your heart beating fast or slow?
- Are you breathing deeply or shallowly?
- Do you have to go to the bathroom?
- Are your muscles tense or loose?
- How does your stomach feel?

How do most people notice these feelings? One of the Eight Sensory Systems, interoception helps us feel or sense the inside of our bodies.

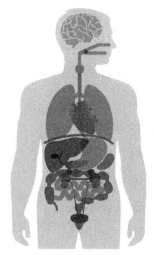

How does the interoceptive system work? Little receptors are found in many of our internal organs and tissues. These little receptors gather information from the insides of our body and send it to the brain. **What messages does the interoceptive system send to the brain?** These messages allow us to feel many important sensations, including hunger, fullness, pain, nausea, need for the bathroom, itch, tickle, and body temperature. Additionally, the signals from our interoceptive system help us to feel our emotions.

How is interoception connected to our emotions? Typically, each emotion feels differently in the body. For example, before speaking in public, the heart may race, the muscles may feel tense, the breathing may become shallow, and the stomach may feel fluttery. These sensations let us know that we are feeling a bit nervous. Without clearly feeling these sensations, it is difficult to identify emotions with clarity.

How does interoception influence self-regulation? When the interoceptive system is working well, the sensations alert us that our internal balance is off and motivates us to take action, to do something that will restore the balance and help us feel more comfortable. For example, if we feel an itch – we scratch it; if we feel full – we stop eating; if we feel anxious – we seek comfort. Interoception underlies our urge for action. If we feel that our internal balance is off, we are motivated to act, to seek immediate relief from the discomfort caused by the imbalance.

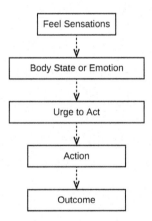

Is interoception important for any other reasons? Interoception underlies many important skills, including:

- decision making
- intuition
- social awareness
- empathy

- perspective taking
- flexibility of thought
- self-awareness
- problem solving

Advance Praise ...

lot of autistic behavior by outlining research on interoception, explaining it in everyday, easy-to-understand language, and guiding the reader on exactly how to access and address interceptive awareness for those whose brains support that happening automatically. Besides being helpful to parents and teachers, Interoception: The Eighth Sensory System *will undoubted change the way occupational therapists practice. In addition, it provides a new lens for mental health professionals to understand and treat the social/emotional difficulties of their clients. Most important, this book allows autistics impacted by interoceptive awareness a respectful new way to understand their difficulties along with practical ideas to become more comfortable inside their own skin as they interface with the world around them. Thank you, Kelly Mahler!"*

– Judy Endow, MSW, autism consultant and author

"Interoception is a groundbreaking, refreshing book bursting with new sensory processing information and outstanding evaluation and treatment techniques. It is a must-read for any clinician working with children and adolescents with sensory processing disorder, autism, ADHD, obesity, and a host of other developmental challenges."

– Kerri L. Hample, OTD, OTR/L

"I was initially skeptical when asked to review this book, but once I picked it up, I could not put it down. As a national expert in behavior and developmental pediatrics and, in particular, communication disorders, I am often asked to review research and literary works in my field. I was immediately taken to the concept of interoception and the simple logic that Mahler applies to a complex area of medical and developmental interest. It is apparent that her eighth sensory system is fully intact and robust given the intuition she has and naturalness she applies to her work. It is a brilliant way to tie complex 'theory of mind' concepts with the 'hidden curriculum,' empathy, intuition and emotional regulation. I am certain that this literary work will appeal to parents, older teens and adults with autism, occupational therapists, psychologists, social workers, speech therapists, and ABA providers. Anyone who evaluates and treats children and adults with autism will benefit from reading Mahler's work. It will most certainly spark the interest of researchers as well to find better assessment tools to measure and improve the quality of life of those on the spectrum."

– Cheryl Tierney, MD, MPH, section chief, Developmental Pediatrics, Penn State Hershey Children's Hospital; president, ABA in PA INITIATIVE

Other AAPC Books Written or Coauthored by Kelly Mahler ...

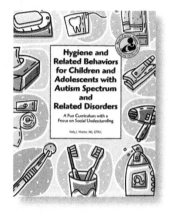

Destination Friendship: Developing Social Skills for Individuals With Autism Spectrum Disorders or Other Social Challenges

Hygiene and Related Behaviors for Children and Adolescents With Autism Spectrum and Related Disorders

Sensory Issues and High-Functioning Autism Spectrum and Related Disorders: Practical Solutions for Making Sense of the World

To order, please go to www.aapcpublishing.net.

11209 Strang Line Rd
Lenexa, KS 66215
www.aapcpublishing.net

CPSIA information can be obtained
at www.ICGtesting.com
Printed in the USA
BVOW06s0450171017
497867BV00017B/184/P